ALIENS AND THE LAW

ALIENS AND THE LAW

SOME LEGAL ASPECTS OF THE
NATIONAL TREATMENT OF ALIENS
IN THE UNITED STATES

WILLIAM MARION GIBSON

THE UNIVERSITY OF NORTH CAROLINA PRESS

CHAPEL HILL

TO

MY PARENTS

FOREWORD

By Richard W. Flournoy

At this period in history, when nationalism and chauvinism have become so pronounced in some quarters, there is a real need of a comprehensive, discriminating, and balanced study of the position and legal rights of aliens resident in our own country. Mr. Gibson's timely study has met this need in a very capable and practical fashion. His work is based, not upon the writings of others, but upon a firsthand examination of original sources, including statutes, treaties, and, in particular, decisions of courts, both state and federal, and awards of arbitral tribunals. His treatment of court decisions and arbitral awards is marked by thoroughness and discrimination. His discussion of taxation problems alone is well worth while.

Mr. Gibson shows that arbitral tribunals have time and again insisted upon the observance by states of a high international standard of justice, and that our own governmental organs, legislative and executive as well as judicial, while occasionally failing to observe this standard, have for the most part observed and promoted it. With reference to the international standard Mr. Gibson quotes at some length from the valuable opinions rendered by Mr. F. K. Nielsen, Commissioner of the United States in the claims arbitrations between the United States and Mexico.

While our own country has carefully maintained its sovereign right to control and limit the immigration of aliens, Mr. Gibson's study shows that it has been very generous in the treatment of those within its gates. In view of the legislation of some states of the Union discriminating against aliens in general or against certain classes of aliens with reference to the acquisition of rights in real property or the pursuit of certain occupations in which they deem it unsafe to have aliens engaged, one might receive the impression that our state governments in general are inclined to be regardless of the legitimate needs of aliens. However, as the author demonstrates by citations of various decisions of state courts, they have not failed to recognize the rights guaranteed to resident aliens, as well as citizens, under the respective constitutions. Moreover, as Mr. Gibson also points out, state legislation has in general been quite liberal toward aliens, and has sometimes even gone beyond the requirements of treaties in the extension of rights to aliens.

No doubt the liberal treatment of aliens, especially under federal laws and treaties, has been due largely to economic considerations and the dictates of commercial policy, but it is also true that such treatment has been influenced to some degree in our country by breadth of view and recognition of the rights of man. It is unfortunate that these considerations have had so little effect in recent years in certain totalitarian states. It is to be hoped that they will come to realize sooner or later that a reasonable degree of humaneness and liberality toward aliens will in the long run represent the best policy.

History has demonstrated that it is natural, and indeed inevitable, for mankind to be divided into separate nations, occupying definite territories and having the character of sovereignty. No doubt human affairs can best be carried on and human needs best served in this way. On the other hand liberal laws and practices governing intercourse between the various states and fair treatment of aliens residing or sojourning within their territories make for the advantage of all concerned. Mr. Gibson's study furnishes valuable in-formation concerning the part taken by our own country in this important matter.

Washington, D. C.
January, 1940.

PREFACE

AN INQUIRY into the determination and protection of personal rights of aliens in the United States has a definite relation to public international law. The major portion of this study has to do with municipal law in the United States relative to aliens. This law is of significance to international law. The municipal law of any state influences the development of international law in two respects. The nature and organization of its municipal law will influence a state's willingness or unwillingness to adhere to a given principle of international law. That is to say, a state will not (possibly may not within the bounds of its own constitutional law) espouse a principle of international law which is incompatible with its municipal legal organization. The second way in which municipal law influences the development of international law is really a corollary of the first. A state which finds its internal legal organization in harmony with a principle of international law is quite likely to use its influence in obtaining international recognition of the principle.

The rights of aliens are defined in customary international law, conventional international law, and municipal law. The first chapter of this study is devoted to a discussion of the personal rights appertaining to an alien by virtue of customary international law. There follows a discussion of treaty provisions into which the United States government has entered which have for their purpose the granting of "national treatment," that is, treatment which is equal to that accorded by a state to its own nationals. The remainder of the study is an inquiry into the municipal legislation and court decisions of the United States, both national and state, relative to the personal rights enjoyed by aliens legally within this country.

All the rights enjoyed by aliens in the United States are not considered. The exclusion of some which they enjoy by virtue of American municipal law has seemed justifiable. The choice is admittedly arbitrary. Consideration has been given only to those rights which have given rise to much litigation and which have caused differences of judicial opinion both as to their nature and as to their extent of enjoyment. It is believed to be more in conformity with the purposes of this study to attempt a clearer statement of disputed matters than to attempt a restatement of the obvious and well-established.

A second self-imposed limitation is that the treatment of aliens by administrative officials has been omitted. This phase of the treatment of aliens has received much attention in books and periodicals, as for example, W. C. Van Vleck's *Administrative Control of Aliens* (1932) and J. P. Clark's *Deportation of Aliens from the United States to Europe* (1931).

For this study, use has been made of standard treatises and authorities on international law. Over one hundred treaties entered into by the United States government have been dealt with in an effort to determine the extent to which this government has bound itself to grant aliens treatment equal to that accorded Americans. Decisions of international tribunals have been investigated and used to determine the personal rights of aliens that have their basis in international law. Material in the archives of the United States Department of State was examined, but nothing was uncovered which could be directly used in the text of this study. Decisions of federal and state courts in the United

States and acts of national and state legislatures have been employed to determine the extent to which personal rights of aliens are protected by municipal law.

The thesis that aliens in the United States are legally entitled to receive more liberal treatment than is required by international law merely, seems to have some significance for the further development of an international legal system.

The preparation of a manuscript is never the work of the author alone. He has consciously and unconsciously leaned heavily upon others. That a debt of gratitude exists is obvious. However, there always stand out a few whose aid has been indispensable. Above all others, the author feels the deepest sense of gratitude to his "chief"—to Professor Robert R. Wilson of Duke University, whose unwearied assistance, counsel, and encouragement have been a constant help throughout the preparation of this study.

There are others to whom the author most gladly acknowledges his gratitude. Miss Mary Covington of the staff of the Duke University Law Library patiently led a neophyte safely through the maze of law books, an accomplishment the greatness of which only she and the author can fully appreciate. Mr. Richard W. Flournoy of the Department of State read the entire manuscript and gave liberally of his learning and experience. Professor Charles Lowndes of the Duke University Law School aided much in the writing of Chapter IV. Dr. Charles B. Hagan of the University of Illinois and Dr. Herman Walker of the United States Department of Agriculture read the manuscript and offered valuable suggestions.

To his wife the author is grateful not only for things spiritual but also for things material. She gladly shouldered the laborious task of preparing the tables which appear in the appendices. W. M. G.

Duke University
1940

CONTENTS

ALIENS AND THE LAW

THE INTERNATIONAL LAW STANDARD
FOR THE TREATMENT OF ALIENS

THE TREATMENT which a state extends to aliens resident within its territory is not determined with finality by the municipal law of that state. International law sets up a minimum standard to which the state must conform. It is not sufficient that the state extend to aliens a treatment equal to that extended its own nationals. The doctrine of national treatment is not a final test of the compatibility of the state's actions with its international responsibilities. The doctrine is merely a point of reference. Instances arise where the international law standard requires that aliens receive treatment which is better than that accorded nationals by the government in whose territory they reside. It is well established in international law that there exist certain fundamental rights which an alien enjoys irrespective of municipal legislation. Any investigation of the subject may well lead to agreement with the Committee of Experts appointed by the League of Nations, who in their report state:

> Some rights are not rights created by states for the benefit of their nationals or of foreigners, namely, the right to life, the right to liberty and the right to own property. The community has simply recognized the existence of these rights and states have mutually undertaken to insure the possibility of enjoying them.[1]

Many publicists and authorities agree that an alien by virtue of international law has the right to life, liberty, and

[1] 20 *American Journal of International Law*, Supp. 182.

property.[2] States are bound by international law to extend at least these rights and the judicial and other methods of protecting them. Some writers are of the opinion that international law grants other rights to aliens, such as freedom of the press, religion, association, and others of this nature.[3] It seems, however, that there still exists too much uncertainty in the law to admit of any convincing proof that international law assures this second group of rights.

It is true that in 1929 the Institute of International Law adopted a code which was believed by that body to be in conformity with the established principles of customary and conventional law.[4] There are some rights concerning which there is doubt whether they are supported by existing customary law. It would be difficult to establish the fact that such rights as freedom of religion, press, and public instruction are protected by customary international law. These rights have ample support in conventional law. Many members of the family of nations are bound by treaties providing for the protection of what may be called the secondary category of rights. But that this category rests equally upon customary law is another question.

There can be no doubt that Article I of the Institute's project is a statement of well-established customary law. But this is the only article which can be based upon customary international law with any certainty.[5]

[2] See F. K. Nielsen, *International Law Applied to Reclamations*, pp. 33-41.

[3] For example, see P. Fauchille, *Traité de Droit International Public*, I, pt. 1, 930; A. Pillet, *Principes de Droit International Privé*, p. 189; J. Thomas, "La Condition des Etrangers et le Droit International," 4 *Revue Générale de Droit International Public* 631.

Article II of the resolutions adopted by the Institute of International Law at New York is as follows: "Il est du devoir de tout Etat de reconnaître, à tout individu, le droit égal au libre exercice, tant public que privé, de toute foi, religion ou croyance, dont la pratique ne sera pas incompatible avec l'ordre public et les bonnes mœurs."—35 *Annuaire*, pt. 2, 117.

[4] 35 *Annuaire*, pt. 2, 117.

[5] Article I: "Il est du devoir de tout Etat de reconnaître à tout individu le droit égal à la vie, à la liberté et à la propriété, et d'accorder à tous, sur son

As indicated above, there are several clearly defined rights which aliens enjoy on the basis of customary international law. These rights are generally referred to as those which are accorded individuals by civilized states. However, international law sits in judgment of the state's actions and does not permit the state to be the sole judge. If the treatment does not measure up to the international law standard, there results an international delinquency for which the delinquent state must make reparation.

This raises the question as to whether or not a state is relieved of all international obligation when it renders national treatment in a given instance. In other words, can a state do anything to aliens so long as it treats its own nationals in the same manner and thereby creates no discrimination? Or, to phrase the question in another manner, if a state may not plead nondiscrimination and thereby relieve itself of all international obligation, are there any rights to which an alien is entitled by virtue of international law regardless of how the state treats its own nationals?

A state does not have the unlimited power to treat aliens as it sees fit. On the contrary, the state is bound by international law to recognize certain rights as belonging to aliens admitted to its territory. It is the practice of states to extend generally the same civil rights to aliens that it extends to nationals. But so far as international law is concerned, the alien is not necessarily entitled to *all* civil rights. For example, a state does not violate any rule of customary law by excluding aliens from ownership of real property, or by excluding them from the exercise of certain professions. But on the other hand, there is also a minimum standard of treatment demanded by international law which cannot be annulled by municipal law and defended by the contention that nationals are likewise denied these rights. In the pro-

---

territoire, pleine et entière protection de ce droit, sans distinction de nationalité, de sexe, de race, de langue ou de religion."—*Ibid.*

tection of that which constitutes a minimum standard of treatment, it is possible for an alien to claim as of right better treatment than that accorded nationals.[6]

In an address before the American Society of International Law, Root referred to the obligation to render such treatment:

Each country is bound to give to the nationals of another country in its territory the benefit of the same laws, the same administration, the same protection, and the same redress for injury which it gives to its own nationals, and neither more nor less: *provided the protection which the country gives to its own citizens conforms to the established standard of civilization.*[7]

The same idea is more forcefully expressed by Commissioner Nielsen in his concurring opinion in the case of *Neer v. Mexico:*

Although there is this clear recognition in international law of the scope of sovereign rights relating to matters that are subject of domestic regulation, it is also clear that the domestic law and the measures employed to execute it must conform to the requirements of the supreme law of members of the family of nations which is international law, and that any failure to meet those requirements is a failure to perform a legal duty, and as such an international delinquency. Hence a strict conformity by authorities of a government with its domestic law is not necessarily conclusive evidence of the observance of legal duties imposed by international law although it may be important evidence on that point.[8]

One of the rights which a state is obligated under international law to extend to aliens is protection against any arbitrary and unfair arrest. A state which imprisons an alien in a manner which is illegal in an international law sense is

---

[6] A. Verdross, "Règles Générales du Droit International de la Paix," 30 *Recueil des Cours de l'Académie* 440.

[7] "The Basis of Protection to Citizens Residing Abroad," 4 *Amer. Journ. of Int'l. Law* 521. Italics mine.

[8] U. S.-Mexico, Gen'l. Claims, Opns. of Comm'rs., 1927, p. 71.

held to have violated international law regardless of the municipal law on the subject. It has been decided that

Under international law a nation has responsibility for the conduct of judicial officers. . . . There must be some ground for depriving a person of his property. He is entitled to be informed of the charge against him if he is arrested on a warrant. Gross mistreatment in connection with arrest and imprisonment is not tolerated, and it has been condemned by international tribunals.[9]

In the case from which this quotation is made, Mexico was held liable for damages because of the treatment of an American by Mexican officials. The offense was held to be compensable not on the ground of any violation of Mexican law, but on the ground that it constituted a violation of international law. This law requires that in the administration of penal laws an alien must be accorded certain rights. There must be some grounds for his arrest; he is entitled to be informed of the charge against him; and he must be given an opportunity to defend himself.[10]

Imprisonment may be justified by international as well as municipal law. But while incarcerated, an alien must be accorded a treatment which is consonant with the standards of international law. Responsibility may not be avoided by the plea that the alien was treated in the same manner as nationals in the particular prison.

Facts with respect to equality of treatment of aliens and nationals may be important in determining the merits of a complaint of mistreatment of an alien. But such equality is not the ultimate test of the propriety of the acts of authorities in the light of international law. The test is, broadly speaking, whether aliens are treated in accordance with ordinary standards of civilization. We do not hesitate to say that the treatment of Roberts was such as to warrant an indemnity on the ground of cruel and inhumane imprisonment.[11]

[9] *Way v. Mexico, ibid.*, 1929, p. 94.
[10] *Chattin v. Mexico, ibid.*, 1927, p. 422.
[11] *Roberts v. Mexico, ibid.*, 1927, p. 100. See also *Faulkner v. Mexico, ibid.*, 1927, p. 86.

Another instance of the improper imprisonment of an alien is to be found in the case of *Díaz v. Guatemala* before the Central American Court of Justice. Although the court concluded that it did not have jurisdiction in this case because the plaintiff had not exhausted his remedies in Guatemala, the opinion contains a very significant statement:

With respect to the first question [Are the plaintiff's injuries protected by international law?] inasmuch as the Nicaraguan nationality of Mr. Fornes Díaz is proven, the court considers that the case comes under its jurisdiction if we look at it exclusively from the standpoint of the nature of the charges, for the fundamental rights and powers of the human individual in civil life are placed under the protection of the principles governing the commonwealth of nations as international rights of man . . .[12]

Not only does international law provide that aliens shall be treated while in prison according to a standard determined by the law, but it also provides that there shall be no excessive delay in bringing the alien prisoner to trial. This is the *ratio decidendi* in the case of *Chazen v. Mexico.*

Mexico had established a zone along her frontier through which it was illegal to carry foreign goods without a permit. Chazen had a permit but was carrying more than his permit allowed. Therefore he was arrested for smuggling. He was held in custody for five days by the customs officials, that is, by administrative officers. Mexican law provided that in this situation such persons should be placed immediately at the disposition of the judicial authorities. The United States government brought suit against Mexico on the grounds that the latter had violated international law in that Chazen was not taken immediately before the judicial authorities, and that his being held in custody by administrative officials constituted an excessive delay forbidden by international law.

[12] Central American Court of Justice, March 6, 1909, 3 *Amer. Journ. of Int'l. Law* 743. This case is not reported in the *Anales* of the court.

The Commission declared that international law sets no time limit for the detention of an accused before being formally remitted to the judicial authorities. Each case must be considered on its merits "bearing in mind the lofty principles of respect for the personal liberty of the individual." The Commission held that under the circumstances five days was too long a delay and therefore Mexico was delinquent in her international obligations.[13]

A state is not only delinquent in its obligations under international law when it permits an excessive delay in bringing an alien to trial; it is also delinquent when it delays too long in capturing and bringing to trial a national who has injured an alien. In such case "the question at issue is whether it reveals a failure of compliance with the general principle of international law requiring authorities to take proper measures to apprehend and punish a person who appears to be guilty of a crime against an alien."[14] In other words, "international law imposes on a nation the obligation to take appropriate steps to prevent infliction of wrongs upon aliens and to employ proper and effective measures to apprehend and punish persons who have committed such wrongs."[15]

It is not enough that a state pass sentence upon one of its nationals for having injured an alien. An international delinquency results if the state does not impose a sentence commensurate with the crime. Commissioner MacGregor, in the case of *Kennedy v. Mexico,* said:

In fact, I think that the international duty which a state has duly to punish those who, within its territory, commit a crime against aliens implies the obligation to impose on the criminal a penalty proportionate to his crime. To punish by imposing a

---

[13] U.S.-Mexico, Gen'l. Claims, Opns. of Comm'rs., 1931, p. 20.

[14] *De Galván v. U.S., ibid.,* 1927, p. 408.

[15] *Janes v. Mexico, ibid.,* 1927, p. 108. See especially the authorities cited, pp. 125 ff.

penalty that does not correspond to the nature of the crime is half punishment or no punishment at all.[16]

International justice is not satisfied "if a Government limits itself to instituting and prosecuting a trial without reaching the point of defining the defendant's guilt and assessing the proper penalty."[17]

A state is under the obligation not only to assess a proper penalty but is also limited by international law in the extent to which it may modify such penalty after it has entered upon enforcement. A Panamanian, having murdered an American, was sentenced to eighteen years and four months. The sentence was first reduced by one-third for good behavior. Then in celebration of the World War Armistice, the government still further reduced the sentence by giving a general amnesty to certain classes of prisoners, among whom was the murderer involved in this case. As a result of these two reductions in the original sentence, the Panamanian national actually served only three years and four months for his crime. The United States brought a claim against Panama on the ground that this was inadequate punishment. It was held that the failure of an individual criminal to serve an adequate term may give rise to an international liability even where the original sentence was adequate. Panama was not relieved of its obligation by the fact that the failure to punish adequately resulted from a general amnesty.[18]

Customary international law recognizes the inviolability of the alien's domicile; that is to say, the right to protection against arbitrary and illegal search and seizure. This right may be a corollary of inviolability of the person or in-

---

[16] *Ibid.*, 1927, p. 289. In this case a Mexican national received a sentence of only two months imprisonment for seriously wounding Kennedy. See also *Putnam v. Mexico, ibid.*, 1927, p. 222.

[17] *Chase v. Mexico, ibid.*, 1929, p. 17.

[18] *Denham v. Panama*, U.S.-Panama, Gen'l. Claims Arb., Hunt's Report, p. 244.

violability of property. Regardless of where one should classify it, it is nevertheless true that such a right is recognized in international customary law.[19]

States are under the international obligation to protect the persons and property of aliens. Once again, it is not a matter of protecting them in the same manner as citizens. The test is whether or not the state exercised "reasonable diligence" as interpreted by international law. In the *Home Insurance Company v. Mexico* the Commission stated that

... the Government of Mexico, in its sovereign capacity owed the duty to protect the persons and property within its jurisdiction by such means as were reasonably necessary to accomplish that end. A failure to discharge that duty resulting in loss or damage to an American national would render it liable here. . . .[20]

In this case, the Commission held that Mexico was not liable because the evidence showed that Mexico had exerted reasonable diligence in according protection. The fact to be emphasized, however, is that the reasonableness of the diligence was determined by an international tribunal functioning under and applying international law.

When a state enters into a contract with an alien and does not fulfill the contract, thereby impairing the alien's property right in the contract, international law provides that the municipal law of the state involved is not the final determiner of the alien's rights. An American bought some Mexican postal money orders which that government refused to cash. The Mexican Agent argued that the claim should be dismissed because of a Mexican statute of limitations. To this argument, Commissioner Nielsen replied:

When questions are raised before an international tribunal, as they have been in the present case, with respect to the appli-

[19] A. Verdross, *op. cit.*, p. 440; P. Fauchille, *op. cit.*, p. 930; J. Thomas, *op. cit.*, p. 631; A. Pillet, *op. cit.*, p. 189.

[20] U.S.-Mexico, Gen'l. Claims, Opns. of Comm'rs., 1927, p. 51.

cation of the proper law in the determination of rights grounded on contractual obligations, it is necessary to have clearly in mind the particular law applicable to the different aspects of the case. The nature of such contractual rights or rights with respect to tangible property, real or personal, which a claimant asserts have been invaded in a given case is determined by the local law that governs the legal effects of the contract or other form of instrument creating such rights. But the responsibility of a respondent Government is determined solely by international law. When it is alleged before an international tribunal that some property rights under a contract have been impaired or destroyed, the tribunal does not sit as a domestic court entertaining a common law action of assumpsit or debt, or some corresponding form of action in the civil law. And in a case involving damages to or confiscation of tangible property, real or personal, inflicted by agencies for which a government is responsible, or by private individuals under conditions rendering a government liable for wrongs inflicted, an international tribunal is not concerned with an action in tort, the merits of which must be determined according to domestic law. The ultimate issue upon which the question of responsibility must be determined in either of these kinds of cases is whether or not there is proof of conduct which is wrongful under international law and which therefore entails responsibility upon a respondent government.[21]

The Commission held that in passing a law relieving the Mexican government of the necessity of cashing the money orders Mexico had violated Cook's property rights in a way contravening international law.

Under international law an alien's property rights are protected against a state's acting in its administrative capacity and not as a party interested directly in the property in question. McNear, an American, sent three cars of wheat to Montemayor, a Mexican grain merchant. When making such a shipment, it is customary in this business for the shipper to draw a draft upon the receiver for the amount of the purchase price. The bill of lading is attached to the

[21] *Cook v. Mexico, ibid.*, 1927, p. 318.

draft. The bank handling the draft does not surrender the bill of lading to the receiver until he has paid the draft. Therefore, title to the grain does not pass to the receiver until he has paid the draft; that is to say, title remains in the shipper until the bank has collected his money for him. In this case, Montemayor was charged by the Mexican government with illegally importing fourteen other cars of wheat, and the government attached the three cars shipped by McNear for revenue due on the fourteen. The United States consul and the bank collecting the draft tried to get the three cars released, but the Mexican court refused on the ground that if they were illegally held the law provided that McNear could obtain their release by bringing a formal action himself before the court. The Claims Commission pointed out that there was unquestionable evidence to the effect that the Mexican court had been informed of the trade practice of shipping under draft with bill of lading attached, and that the court had ample opportunity to acquaint itself with the correctness of this information. The opinion of the Commission was:

From that moment [when the court had been informed of the trade practice] their retention of the wheat constitutes a violation of a rule that is of fundamental importance to commerce and with which they should have been familiar. For this violation the Commission holds that Mexico must be responsible under international law, notwithstanding that possibly McNear might have had his rights recognized, if he had brought a formal action before the court.

The Commission went on to point out that since there was no evidence brought before it to indicate that it was necessary to seize and sell these three cars for nonpayment of duty, the goods were wrongfully taken and McNear could not be required to make formal application for their release no matter what the Mexican law said on the subject.[22]

[22] *McNear v. Mexico, ibid.,* 1929, p. 68.

International law protects an alien's property which is in the custody of a trustee as a result of bankruptcy proceedings. An American railroad company operating in Mexico became bankrupt and the Mexican government attached four locomotives and placed them in the custody of a bankruptcy trustee (*síndico*). In Mexico, as elsewhere, the trustee cannot be considered an official of the government; he acts as representative of the creditors. In countries with bankruptcy legislation such as the Mexican code contains, direct responsibility for what happens to the bankrupt estate lies not with the government but with those in whose care it is placed by the government. However, the Claims Commission pointed out that, "though the direct responsibility for what befalls such attached goods does not rest with the courts and the government they represent, because these are not the custodians, a heavy burden of indirect responsibility lies upon them."

While in the care of the trustee, the locomotives were kept in open yards, a prey to the elements. In addition to the natural deterioration which would result from such a situation, vandals had removed or injured so many important parts that the locomotives were reduced to a practically worthless condition. No investigation of the vandalism was made by any prosecuting attorney, no account was required from the trustee by the court, and nothing was done to have the bankruptcy proceedings terminated. In the light of these facts the Commission was of the opinion that

Even if there was not willful neglect of duty, there doubtless was an insufficiency of governmental action so far short of international standards that every reasonable and impartial man would readily recognize its insufficiency. Whether this insufficiency proceeded from the law or from deficient execution of the law is immaterial. The court at Monterrey can not plead innocence; having constrained private individuals to leave their property in the hands of others, having allowed unknown men to spoil and destroy this property, and not having taken any action whatsoever to punish the culprits, to obtain indemnification, to have the custodians removed or replaced, or to bring the bankruptcy to an end, it rendered Mexico indirectly liable for what occurred.

The Commission decided that under international law these circumstances presented a case for which a government must be held liable.[23]

International law sets standards of protection for aliens' property as against individual violation as well as governmental. Moreover this protection includes the obligation to prevent as well as to repair illegal violations of property. Ermerins and his family were living in Vera Cruz. There developed in the town such a feeling against Americans that Ermerins and his family left there. The day following their departure the house was looted. The United States government brought a claim against Mexico for this violation of property. The Commission agreed with the United States agent's argument that, under the circumstances in the case, international law holds Mexico responsible for the looting because of the latter's failure to provide adequate protection.

Especially in view of the fact that the house was situated just across the street from police headquarters and the Alcalde's office, the Commission is of the opinion that a crime of this nature could not have taken place if the authorities of the town had properly fulfilled their duty to afford protection to the property of Ermerins, which they must have known would be exposed to danger under the circumstances prevailing at the time.[24]

In view of the fact that international customary law protects aliens in the enjoyment of the property rights discussed above, it is to be expected that the law would have some provision for the alien's ownership of property. It is

[23] *Venable v. Mexico, ibid.,* 1927, p. 331.
[24] *Ermerins v. Mexico, ibid.,* 1929, p. 219.

provided for in the first article of the Institute's draft convention[25] and recognized by implication in the fifth article of the Pan-American convention of 1933.[26] Publicists are quite unanimous in declaring such a right to exist in international law. There seems to be no question or dispute among the writers and authorities that an alien has the right to the ownership of what in Anglo-American terminology is called personal property.[27] The right to own immovables, however, is a limited one. A state may, without violating international law, forbid aliens to own real estate, or may permit them ownership under limitations and restrictions.[28]

The problem of a state's right to take property without indemnification has occasioned a very sharp debate between Sir John Fischer Williams[29] and A. P. Fachiri.[30] The former maintains the position that international law does not require the state to indemnify an alien for property taken if taken under a law which applies equally to nationals of the confiscating country. Fachiri contends that this is in error. He adheres to the position that international law requires indemnification regardless of how the municipal law affects nationals. Undoubtedly Fachiri has much the more convincing argument. Certainly the United States government's attitude upon this matter is in conformity with Fachiri. Our history contains many instances of demands for indemnification being successfully made.[31]

[25] See above, note 5.
[26] Pan-American Convention on the Rights and Duties of States, signed at Montevideo, Dec. 26, 1933, *U.S. Session Laws*, 1935, p. 707.
[27] A. Pillet, *op. cit.*, p. 185.
[28] J. P. Niboyet, *Manuel de Droit International Privé*, p. 302; H. Kelsen, "Théorie Générale du Droit International Public," 42 *Recueil des Cours de l'Académie* 249.
[29] "International Law and the Property of Aliens," *Brit. Yr. Bk. of Int'l. Law*, 1928, pp. 1-30. [30] *Ibid.*, 1929, pp. 32-55.
[31] *Jonas King*, J. B. Moore, *A Digest of International Law*, VI, 262; *Hatton v. Mexico*, U.S.-Mexico, Gen'l. Claims, Opns. of Comm'rs., 1929, p. 6; *American Bottle Co. v. Mexico*, ibid., 1929, p. 162; *Putegnat Heirs v. Mexico*, J. B. Moore, *International Arbitrations*, p. 3718; *Ashmore v. China*, ibid., p. 1857.

The right to protection of person and property carries with it the right to equal treatment in tribunals charged with this protection. If, in troubled times, the courts of a state are not functioning, thereby denying the alien an opportunity to obtain protection of person and property, the state does not cease to have the obligation of protection. An alien is entitled to reclamation should he suffer any injury during such time. The offending state may not absolve itself from this responsibility on the ground that the injury was suffered at a time when the state was incapable of extending normal protection.[32] Moreover, it is a violation of international law if a state, in peace times, refuses or limits the juridic protection of aliens either in its courts or at the hands of its administrative officers. Excessive delays are also contrary to the law of nations. In short, "in the matter of administrative and judicial procedure, nationals of foreign states are, by virtue of international law assimilated, in principle, to nationals."[33] Certain minor restrictions upon aliens are permitted, such as a deposit of money and similar requirements which are designed not to interfere with giving the alien justice, but which have for their purpose the prevention of the alien's abuse of his rights.

There exists very respectable opinion that international law requires a state to permit an alien legally within its jurisdiction to have the right to gainful employment. That the United States gives wide recognition to this principle is evidenced by many bipartite treaties of commerce into which it has entered providing for this.[34] Although the right to engage in a gainful occupation is recognized by international law, it is not unlimited. As Kelsen points out, the state may exclude aliens from the exercise of certain professions and trades.[35] In doing so, the state incurs no

[32] A. Pillet, op. cit., p. 189.
[33] H. Kelsen, op. cit., p. 250.   [34] See Chap. II.
[35] Op. cit., p. 253. See also, C. C. Hyde, International Law Chiefly as Interpreted and Applied by the United States, I, 357 ff.

liability provided such exclusion was not patently arbitrary and manifestly unreasonable. It would seem that any exclusion is not prohibited by international law if it can meet tests similar to tests which an American municipal court would utilize in determining what is a proper exercise of the police power.

The nature of the foregoing discussion naturally leads one to the question of whether or not international law makes possible situations in which aliens may demand as of right a treatment which is better than the treatment accorded by a state to its own nationals. The answer to this question is that the alien may within a limited sphere receive as of right better than national treatment. The United States-Mexican Claims Commission had occasion to answer this question directly.

An American national, Hopkins, had purchased some money orders under authority of the Huerta revolutionary government. When Carranza established his government *de jure,* the money orders issued by the Huerta government were rescinded. The United States government entered a claim on behalf of Hopkins with the Claims Commission for this money. The Mexican government took the position that the treaty of 1923 did not embrace such a claim because it gave Hopkins better treatment than a Mexican similarly situated received under the Mexican municipal law. To this contention the Commission replied:

If it be argued that under the provisions of the treaty of 1923 as construed by this commission the claimant Hopkins enjoys both rights and remedies against Mexico which it withholds from its own citizens under its municipal laws, the answer is that it not infrequently happens that under the rules of international law applied to controversies of an international aspect a nation is required to accord to aliens broader and more liberal treatment than it accords to its own citizens under its municipal law. The reports of decisions made by arbitral tribunals long prior to the treaty of 1923 contain many such instances. There is no ground to object that this amounts to a discrimination by a nation against its own citizens in favor of aliens. It is not a question of discrimination but a question of difference in their respective rights and remedies. The citizens of a nation may enjoy many rights which are withheld from aliens, and, conversely, under international law aliens may enjoy rights and remedies which the nation does not accord to its own nationals.[36]

Additional evidence of the fact that the United States government recognizes the possibility of better than national treatment is to be found in Secretary of State Bayard's communication to Buck, Minister to Peru, in which the Secretary said:

It cannot be admitted that in every case the rights of a foreigner in that country [Peru] may be measured by the extent of the protection to person and property which a citizen might obtain. . . . It not infrequently happens that citizens of a country are compelled to endure injuries which would afford ample basis for international intervention if they were inflicted on foreigners.[37]

To offer a complete statement of the American attitude upon the problem of whether aliens may obtain by virtue of international law treatment better than that of nationals, it is necessary to mention the 1933 Pan-American Convention on the Rights and Duties of States to which the United States government is a party. Article IX of the convention provides that "nationals and foreigners are under the same protection of the law and the national authorities and foreigners may not claim rights other or more extensive than those of nationals."[38]

This provision is obviously in conflict with the principles that have been discussed above. International law, as is the

---

[36] *Hopkins v. Mexico*, U.S.-Mexico, Gen'l. Claims, Opns. of Comm'rs., 1927, p. 42.   [37] J. B. Moore, *Digest*, VI, 252.
[38] *U. S. Session Laws*, 1935, p. 707.

case with any other law, must meet the test of time and practice. The convention has not been so tested. Regardless of the merit of such a provision as a factor in international peace and relations, it is a conventional departure from an impressive and well-established body of law. Whether it will be able to stand in the face of such opposition may well be doubted.

There are certain minimum standards of treatment that are required by international law to which states must conform under penalty of international responsibility.[39] There is nothing to prevent a state from affording a treatment which is superior to this. The purpose of the foregoing discussion has been to explain the nature of the minimum standards. It is when a state falls below the requirements of the minimum standards of treatment that the problem of "better than national treatment" may arise. The statement has been made above that there is the possibility of an alien's receiving better than national treatment within a limited sphere. The limitation is the minimum standards required by the law. It is suggested that confusion and the appearance of injustice to nationals result from speaking of "better than national treatment." A national may receive less favorable treatment from his government than an alien would receive when the state interferes with the minimum standards. However, the basis for the treatment of the national is municipal law while the basis for the alien is international law. Therefore, their respective treatments are not comparable, and to speak of "better than national treatment" is to use a meaningless phrase.

[39] P. A. Steinbach, *Untersuchungen zum Internationalen Fremdenrecht, passim*.

II

NATIONAL TREATMENT PROVISIONS
IN UNITED STATES TREATIES

CUSTOMARY international law prescribes and protects a comparatively restricted group of rights. By virtue of national treatment provisions in treaties, aliens have been accorded a wider variety of rights than they possess under customary international law. The United States government has entered into many treaties containing such provisions. The types of treaties in which they are to be found are treaties of amity, commerce and navigation; treaties of friendship and peace; consular conventions; and several multipartite conventions on such subjects as industrial property, trademarks, copyright, aliens and air navigation. These provisions may be divided into three categories. The first category relates to what may be termed personal rights and privileges. The second deals with matters relative to goods. The third has for its purpose the extension of national treatment to vessels.

Although this inquiry is concerned primarily with the nature of the alien's personal rights or, more properly termed, civil rights in this country, it is necessary to give passing attention to the national treatment provisions relative to shipping and commerce that are found in the treaties. It is for this reason that the latter portion of the chapter has to do with this type of provision. Unfortunately, there is a paucity of writing upon the provisions having to do with national treatment in civil rights. Most of the writing is concerned with the controversies brought about by the national treatment provisions relative to shipping. This phase of the treaties is bound up with the problems of commercial reciprocity and most-favored-nation treatment. An attempt will be made to explain the nature of all the national treatment provisions, those having to do with civil rights and those relative to shipping and commerce.

The advantages to be obtained from entering into treaties of this type are obvious. Discrimination against aliens is an old problem. With the increase of commerce and international trade, and the resulting increase in the numbers of aliens present in the various countries of the world, this unhappy situation became acute. Two alternatives presented themselves. The nations of the world could have continued their inequitable treatment, with the resulting discouragement of international trade and commerce. The desirability and value of foreign trade made such a policy unprofitable. To permit and foster this type of economic activity, it was evident that a change of policy toward aliens was necessary. Governments realized that if they wished to facilitate their international commerce by securing greater advantages and benefits for their nationals abroad they had to offer the governments of other countries a *quid pro quo*. This resulted in what is known as national treatment of aliens; that is to say, in certain stipulated matters a given government will put the nationals of the other state upon equal footing with its own nationals.

When the North American colonies achieved their independence from Great Britain, they were faced for a long time with the problems of commerce. These problems were acute because of the fact that Europe favored a commercial policy which made it difficult for the Americans to participate in the commerce of the world.[1] In a letter to Secretary Livingston, dated August 3, 1783, John Adams said:

[1] For an excellent account of these problems and the way in which the United States government met them see T. W. Page, "The Earlier Commercial Policy of the United States," 10 *Journal of Political Economy* 161-192.

The fiscal systems of the powers of Europe have such an ill influence on commerce, that they deserve the serious attention of congress and their ministers, whenever they have under consideration a treaty with any foreign power. In conversation yesterday with M. d'Asp, the *chargé des affaires* of Sweden, I inquired of him what imposts were payable in their ports upon the importation and exportation of merchandises, and observed to him that I had lately seen in the gazettes that the king had taken off certain duties upon the importation of merchandises from America, in Swedish ships. He agreed that such a thing had been done. This ought to alarm us. All the powers of Europe who are called neutral, have felt a sudden increase of their navigation in the course of the late war, and the profits they have made have excited a desire to augment it still further. If they should generally exact duties of our ships and none of their own, upon the importation of our produce, this will be as great a discouragement to our navigation as it will be to theirs. Whether this has been attended to in the treaty with Sweden, I do not know, for I have not seen it. But it ought to be carefully considered by those who negotiate the treaties with Denmark and Portugal, the Emperor and Empress, and all other powers. We have a good right to insist that no distinction shall be made in their ports between their ships and ours; that we should pay in their ports no higher duties than they pay in ours.[2]

Undoubtedly the unfavorable position of the United States in world trade did much to direct the government's treaty negotiators toward the achievement of national treatment, particularly in matters of commerce and navigation. That the commercial treaties into which the United States government entered did contain national treatment provisions is quite true, but they dealt predominantly with commercial matters and comparatively few of the provisions related to civil rights of nationals while in the jurisdiction of the other contracting party. It was not until the fourth decade of the nineteenth century that national treatment

[2] C. F. Adams, *Works of John Adams*, VIII, 130.

provisions relative to civil rights of individuals appeared in American treaties to any great extent. Since that time there has been a gradual expansion of provisions relative to national treatment in civil rights and in matters of commerce and navigation.[3]

PROVISIONS RELATIVE TO PERSONAL RIGHTS OR PRIVILEGES[4]

1. *The right to enter, travel, sojourn:*—American treaties extend national treatment to aliens in matters of acquiring real property, protection of persons and property, religious freedom, various provisions for carrying on business and commerce, and other such privileges as are discussed below.

For the utmost enjoyment of national treatment in the matters listed immediately above, travel and sojourn in the territory of the foreign country would be necessary. However, the granting of national treatment in these matters does not imply the right to travel and sojourn in such territory. The possibilities for conflict between such an implication and the immigration policies of the governments concerned are great. Immigration policies are so predominantly a domestic matter that they should not be impliedly modified by conventional law. Any modification of such policies must be done by expression rather than implication. Therefore, in about thirty of the treaties considered there is a specific provision to the effect that the citizens of one contracting party "shall be permitted to enter, sojourn, settle and reside in all parts of the territory of the other contracting party." But in most of these treaties such a broad statement is narrowed by qualifications which make it clear that the contracting parties did not intend to surrender their right to impose restrictions conflicting with the right to

---

[3] For the commercial aspect of this development see W. McClure, "A New American Commercial Policy," *Columbia Univ. Studies in Hist., Econ. and Public Law*, Vol. CXIV.

[4] In the remainder of this chapter citations of treaty provisions are not placed in footnotes. See complete table in Appendix A, below.

travel and sojourn. The grant is not as great as it might appear to be at first glance.

In the treaties with Peru (1851), Nicaragua (1867) and San Salvador (1870) the parties bind themselves to extend to citizens of the other party the same security in these matters that is enjoyed by the natives of the country in which the alien finds himself, on condition, however, that the alien "duly observe the laws and ordinances" of the country. The treaty with Spain (1902), although extending the right to enter and travel, specifically reserves the right of expulsion.

The treaties that have been entered into since the World War contain an innovation in that they provide for the right of transit, provided such persons and goods are admissible under municipal law in the first place. A typical provision of this type stipulates:

> There shall be complete freedom of transit through the territories including the territorial waterways of each of the High Contracting Parties on the routes most convenient for international transit, by rail, navigable waterway, and canal, other than the Panama Canal and waterways and canals which constitute international boundaries of the United States, to such persons and goods coming from or going through the territories of the other High Contracting Party, except such persons as may be forbidden admission into its territories or goods of which the importation may be prohibited by law. Persons and goods in transit shall not be subjected to any transit duty, or to any unnecessary details or restrictions, and shall be given national treatment as regards charges, facilities and all other matters.

2. *The right to engage in work:*—The provisions of earlier treaties relative to commercial activity extended national treatment to aliens primarily in navigation. This is to be expected because the commercial activity of aliens in a foreign country was chiefly concerned with bringing goods to that country. The establishment of enterprises by aliens for handling goods after they entered the foreign country

was to come later. Therefore, these earlier treaties provided that the citizens and subjects of each contracting party "may frequent the coasts and countries of the other with their ships and reside and trade there in all kinds of produce, manufacturing and merchandise." In the enjoyment of this privilege, they were extended all the rights and exemptions in navigation and commerce which native citizens enjoyed. However, these treaties usually excluded aliens from the coasting trade. It should be noted that the treaty with San Salvador (1850) extended national treatment in mining, and this provision was renewed in the treaty of 1870 with that country.

During the second half of the nineteenth century additional stipulations as to the type of business in which aliens might engage on an equal basis with nationals made their appearance. Beginning with the treaty with Peru (1851), there are several agreements extending to the nationals of each party the right "to open retail stores and shops under the same municipal and police regulations as native citizens."

The Siamese treaty of 1920 has a provision whereby the nationals of the contracting parties may, within the territories of the other, "carry on trade, wholesale and retail, engage in religious, educational and charitable work."

The treaties subsequent to the World War permit citizens of the other contracting party "to engage in every trade, vocation, manufacturing industry and profession not reserved exclusively to nationals of the country."[5] Several of these postwar treaties make an even more extensive list of activities. For example, the treaty with Norway (1928) provides that "the nationals of each of the high contracting parties shall be permitted . . . to engage in professional, scientific, religious, philanthropic, manufacturing and com-

[5] On the exclusion of aliens from certain vocations, see below, pp. 123 ff.

mercial work of every kind without interference; to carry on every form of commercial activity which is not forbidden by local law." Here again the right is subject to restriction by unilateral action through municipal law.

The Pan-American Aviation Convention of 1928 extends equality of treatment in the matter of the establishment and operation of aerodromes.

3. *The right to acquire real property:*—There are two types of provisions relating to real estate to be found in American treaties. The first type provides that the nationals of the other party may acquire buildings of one kind or another, whereas the other type specifically provides for the acquisition of land as well as buildings. The earlier treaties extended only the right to obtain buildings. It was not until the treaty with San Salvador in 1850 that provisions for the acquisition of lands as well as buildings made their appearance.

It is instructive to note that the earlier treaties not only confined their provisions to the acquisition of buildings, but further modified and circumscribed this right by providing that the nationals of the two contracting parties could "hire and possess houses and ware-houses *for the purpose of their commerce.*" [Italics mine.] Prior to 1850, there were only two treaties which intended the right to include buildings for dwelling purposes as well as for commercial purposes.

Likewise, it was not until after 1850 that the treaty provisions extending the right to acquire land as well as buildings made their appearance. From this date it is not uncommon to find the provisions relating to real property concerned with the acquisition of buildings and lands. A typical provision of this nature is to be found in the treaty with Japan of 1911 which provides that the citizens of each party shall have the right "to own or lease and occupy houses, manufacturies, warehouses, and shops . . . to lease land for residential and commercial purposes. . . ."[6]

It is to be noted that this provision permitted the owning as well as leasing of buildings for purposes of residence and commerce, whereas lands for residential and commercial purposes could only be leased. But in the postwar treaties there are more extensive specifications of the purposes to which land acquired by aliens can be put. For instance, the Polish treaty of 1931, a typical postwar treaty, provides that "the nationals of each of the High Contracting Parties shall be permitted . . . to own, erect or lease and occupy appropriate buildings and to lease lands for residential, scientific, religious, philanthropic, manufacturing, commercial and mortuary purposes."

4. *Protection against illegal search and seizure:*—Most of the treaties which make any provision for the protection of the alien's enjoyment of and security in his buildings and records extend this protection by such provisions as found in the Austrian treaty of 1928. There it is stipulated:

> The dwellings, manufacturies, shops and other places of business, and all premises thereto appertaining of the nationals of each of the High Contracting Parties in the territories of the other . . . shall be respected. It shall not be allowable to make a domiciliary visit to, or search of any such buildings and premises, or there to examine or inspect books, papers, or accounts, except under the conditions and in conformity with the forms prescribed by the laws, ordinances, and regulations for nationals.

Three of the treaties (Bolivia, 1858; Peru, 1870; Peru, 1887) extend this protection only to visit and search of buildings and make no mention of whether or not the books, papers, and accounts of aliens may be inspected without orders from the proper officials.

On the other hand, the treaties with Haiti (1864) and

---

[*] Court interpretation of this type of provision is considered below at pp. 52 ff.

Peru (1851) make no mention of protection against arbitrary domiciliary visits and searches, but confine their stipulations to the statement that "there shall be no examination or inspection of the books, papers, or accounts of the citizens of either country residing within the jurisdiction of the other without the legal order of a competent tribunal or judge."

5. *Protection of persons and property:*[7]—Provisions making the specific commitment that the nationals of each country shall enjoy within the territories of the other a protection of their persons and property which is equal to the protection extended by the country to its own nationals did not appear until the Belgian and Sicilian treaties of 1845. All treaties preceding these two merely provided that the citizens of each of the parties shall receive "special protection," or "full and perfect protection," for their persons and property, and that was the full extent of the provisions.

The earliest American treaty containing a protection provision, that with Great Britain of 1794, extended just to "merchants and traders" a "most complete protection and security for their commerce." However, this type of provision was unique. The treaties entered into between 1794 and 1845 contained provisions comparable in substance to the following:

Both contracting parties promise and engage, formally to give their special protection to the persons and property of the citizens of each other, of all occupations, who may be in the territories subject to the jurisdiction of the one or the other, transient or dwelling therein . . . [Colombia, 1824]

As mentioned above, the Belgian and Sicilian treaties of 1845 were the first agreements which made specific provi-

---

[7] As to the nature of this form of treaty provision and the protection it affords in the United States, see P. Q. Wright, "The Enforcement of International Law through Municipal Law in the United States," *Univ. of Ill. Studies in the Social Sciences,* V, 78 ff.

sion for the protection of persons and property of aliens and placed this protection upon the basis of national treatment. Treaties containing any provision relative to this matter entered into during the second half of the nineteenth century may be exemplified by the treaty with Italy (1871). In this treaty it was provided that

The citizens of each of the High Contracting Parties shall receive in the States and territories of the other the most constant protection and security for their persons and property, and shall enjoy in this respect the same rights and privileges as are or shall be granted to natives.

The postwar treaties contain an innovation. For example, the treaty with Poland (1931) provides that

The nationals of each High Contracting Party shall receive within the territories of the other, upon submitting to conditions imposed upon its nationals, the most constant protection and security for their persons and property, *and shall enjoy in this respect that degree of protection that is required by international law.* [Italics mine.]

In more recent years, beginning with the Italian treaty of 1913, national treatment is being extended to nationals of one party who are heirs, dependents, or relatives of a person injured or killed in the territory of the other party. In other words, where there are any national, state, or provincial laws establishing civil liability for injuries or for death, and giving to relatives, heirs, and dependents a right of action or a pecuniary benefit, the same right of action or pecuniary benefit is to be given to the alien or his beneficiaries. This benefit is to be extended to such persons regardless of their alienage or residence outside of the territory where the injury occurred.

The postwar treaties have a "due process of law" provision whereby the governments of the contracting states may not arbitrarily take property without creating an international responsibility and obligation. These treaties bind the parties so that the property of the aliens may be taken only by due process of law and after payment of just compensation.

In many treaties there are provisions concerning military service of aliens. These provisions contain certain stipulations for the protection of alien property which may logically be discussed at this time.

Only two of the treaties (Two Sicilies, 1855; Tonga, 1886) specifically prohibit the contracting parties from quartering their troops in the houses occupied by nationals of the other party. The Peruvian (1887) and the Bolivian (1858) treaties extend the following protection to property of nationals of the other contracting party in case of war between them. They provide:

. . . nor shall they be liable to any embargo, or to be detained with their vessels, cargoes, merchandise, goods or effects for any military expedition, or for any purpose whatever, without being allowed therefor a full and sufficient indemnification, which shall in all cases be agreed upon and paid in advance.

The Pan-American Convention on the Status of Aliens (1928) has a provision relative to the rights of the contracting parties to demand the services of aliens within their borders. By this convention

foreigners may not be obliged to perform military service; but those foreigners who are domiciled, unless they prefer to leave the country, may be compelled, under the same conditions as nationals, to perform police, fire protection, or militia duty for the protection of the place of their domicile against natural catastrophies or dangers not resulting from war.

In the event of war between the contracting parties many of the treaties provide for the protection of nationals of one party found within the jurisdiction of the other. Aliens are usually allowed a period of time to dispose of their property and depart from the country. However, if they choose to remain in the foreign country, it is usually provided that they shall have the privilege of remaining and continuing in their trade and employment "without any manner of interruption." In the event they elect to remain and conduct themselves peaceably, their goods and effects, of whatever description they may be, whether in their own custody or intrusted to individuals or to the state, shall not be liable to seizure or sequestration, nor to any other charges or demands than those which may be made upon the like effects or property belonging to native citizens.

6. *Protection of trade-marks and patents:*—American treaties containing provisions for the mutual protection of trade-marks, patents, and copyrights did not appear until the last quarter of the nineteenth century. Of the treaties considered, the first to give attention to this subject was the multipartite convention on industrial property of 1883. Article II of this convention provided that

The subjects or citizens of each of the contracting States shall enjoy, in all the other States of the Union, so far as concerns patents for inventions, trade or commercial marks, and the commercial names, the advantages that the respective laws thereof at present accord, or shall afterwards accord to the subjects or citizens. In consequence they shall have the same protection as the latter, and the same legal recourse against all infringements of their rights, under reserve of complying with the formalities and conditions imposed upon subjects or citizens by the domestic legislation of each State.

The Danish treaty of 1892, while extending national treatment in this matter, sees to it that the nationals of one state may not, under the guise of national treatment, obtain in the other state better treatment than they would at home. This treaty specifically provides "that in the United States the subjects of Denmark, and in Denmark, the citizens of the United States of America, can not enjoy these rights to a greater extent or for a longer period of time than in their native country."

For the enjoyment of equal protection relative to patents and trade-marks, the various conventions provide that when nationals of one state seek the protection of other states they must comply with the laws of registration that govern the patent and trade-mark rights of the nationals of the other state. But the Pan-American copyright convention of August 11, 1910, removes, so far as copyrights are concerned, "the necessity of complying with any of the formalities, provided always there shall appear in the work a statement that indicates the reservation of the property right." One other Pan-American provision should be mentioned, the convention of August 20, 1910, which provides in Article VIII that "the ownership of a patent of invention comprises the right to enjoy the benefits thereof, and the right to assign or transfer it in accordance with the laws of the country."

7. *Internal charges and taxes:*—At this time it is proposed to consider only those taxes and charges other than duties, tonnage, and such charges, and those taxes connected with international commercial activity. The taxes which normally run during peace times may be dismissed with the brief statement that the treaties are uniform in providing that the nationals of one party may remain within the territories of the other "without being subjected as to their persons or property, or with regard to the exercise of their trade or business, to any taxes, whether general or local, or to any imposts or conditions of any kind other or more onerous than those which are or may be imposed upon natives or upon the subjects of the most favored nation."

The treaties provide that in time of war aliens shall not be subjected to any other charges, contributions, or taxes than such as are paid by citizens of the states in which they reside. There are also provisions prohibiting the states from demanding forced loans from the nationals of the other contracting party within their territories. Attention is directed to the fact that this protection is found only in treaties with South American countries, with the exception of the treaty with the Two Sicilies of 1855. These South American treaties were entered into during the nineteenth century. It seems that there has been a change of heart in this matter in the western hemisphere because of the fact that the Pan-American Convention of February 20, 1928, provides that "foreigners are obliged to make ordinary and extraordinary contributions, *as well as forced loans,* always provided that such measures apply to the population generally." [Italics mine.] Treaties with the Orange Free State (1871) and the Swiss Confederation (1850), while stipulating that aliens shall be free from personal military service, yet make these aliens liable to the pecuniary or material contributions which may be required, by way of compensation, from citizens of the country where they reside, who are exempt from the said service." On the other hand, the Japanese treaty of 1894 makes a specific exemption from all contributions imposed in lieu of personal services.

8. *Access to courts; punishments:*—Provisions concerning access to courts in most treaties contain three elements. The first is that the contracting parties engage to leave free and open their tribunals of justice to nationals of the other contracting party "on the same terms which are usual and customary with the natives or citizens of the country in which they may be." The second element extends to aliens the right to employ such advocates, solicitors, agents, and others as they may judge proper in all their trials at law and upon the same footing as nationals of the state wherein they are. The third element gives these aliens or their agents "free opportunity to be present at the decisions and sentences of the tribunals in all cases which concern them, and likewise at the taking of all examinations and evidence which may be exhibited in the said trials."

In seventeen of the treaties, only the first two elements mentioned above are to be found in the provisions relative to access to courts. On the other hand, the treaty with the Netherlands (1782) does not make any specific grant of access to courts, but does extend to the citizens and subjects of each party the right "to employ such advocates, attorneys, notaries, solicitors, or factors as they shall judge proper." The postwar instruments provide that "the nationals of each of the high contracting parties shall enjoy freedom of access to the courts of justice of the other on conforming to the local laws, as well for the prosecution as for the defense of their rights, and in all degrees of jurisdiction established by law."

The Spanish treaty of 1795 contains a unique provision. It requires that the courts of the two parties shall be open on a basis of equality for cases arising between the nationals of one state and the nationals of the other. In this the provision makes no departure from other provisions relative to access to courts. But it is further provided that nationals of either country may enter suits in the courts of the other party against "any other persons whatsoever, who may take refuge therein; and the proceedings and sentences of the said courts shall be the same as if the contending parties had been subjects or citizens" of the state wherein the case is tried.

Very few of the treaties contain any specific provision relative to imprisonment. Only the Peruvian treaties of 1851, 1870, and 1887, and the Bolivian treaty of 1858 make any mention of this matter. The Peruvian treaties provide that

Said citizens shall not be liable to imprisonment without formal commitment under a warrant signed by a legal authority, except in cases *flagrantis delicti;* and they shall in all cases be brought to a magistrate, or other legal authority, for examination, within twenty-four hours after arrest; and if not so examined, the accused shall forthwith be discharged from custody. Said citizens when detained in prison, shall be treated during their imprisonment with humanity, and no unnecessary severity shall be exercised toward them.

Article XIII of the Bolivian treaty (1858) subjects nationals of one country engaged in political matters in the other country to the same measures of punishment and prevention as nationals of the country where they reside.

9. *Inheritance and transmission of property:*—Treaty provisions concerning the inheritance and transmission of property virtually discontinue the operation of the common law so far as concerns nationals of the contracting parties in the United States. It is true that municipal legislation in most of the states of the United States has modified the common law by removing the disabilities that the common law placed upon aliens in the matter of real property, but the existence of treaty provisions having the same effect places the rights of aliens upon an international basis and thereby protects them against the vicissitudes of municipal legislation.[8]

Under the common law aliens had no right to inherit or bequeath real property or to remove the proceeds of the sale of such property from the country. Generally speaking, the treaty provisions extend to nationals of the contracting parties the right to bequeath and to inherit real as well as personal property found within the jurisdiction of the other contracting party. Likewise, aliens are given the right to dispose of their property as they see fit and to remove the proceeds thereof from the country. In all these matters they are to be subjected to no other or higher charges or duties than are paid by nationals of the country in like circumstances.

The transmission and inheritance of personal property by aliens does not offer any great problem. Under the com-

---

[8] See A. K. Kuhn, "The Supremacy of Treaties over State Laws in Respect to the Intestate Estates of Aliens," 26 *Amer. Journ. of Int'l. Law* 348-351.

mon law, they were able to dispose of their personalty very much as they pleased. A typical provision relative to this type of property is found in the treaty with Württemberg of 1844, which stipulates that

The citizens or subjects of each of the contracting parties shall have power to dispose of their personal property within the States of the other, by testament, donation, or otherwise, and their heirs, legatees, and donees, being citizens or subjects of the other contracting party shall succeed to their said personal property, and may take possession thereof, either by themselves, or by others acting for them, and dispose of the same at their pleasure, paying such duties only as the inhabitants of the country where the said property lies, shall be liable to pay in like cases.

Treaty provisions of this nature contribute very little, if anything, to an expansion of alien rights under common law.

The provisions in most of the treaties into which the United States government has entered provide that if heirs are prevented from inheriting real property because of their character as aliens they shall be allowed either a "reasonable time" or some specified period of years to dispose of the real property they otherwise would have inherited and into the possession of which they could have entered had they not been aliens. During this period of time, the alien heirs are permitted to sell the real property and remove the proceeds of the sale "without molestation, and exempt from all rights of detraction on the part of the government of the respective States."[9] In other words, if an alien inherits real property in one of the states of the United States which does not permit aliens to hold such property, he does not lose his in-

[9] Several earlier treaties, particularly those with the Hanseatic Republics, abolished the *droit d'aubaine* and the *droit de détraction*. "This practice of the princes has fallen into disuse and the exemption has crystallized into a principle of international law and is, therefore, omitted from present-day treaties."—C. E. Hill, *Leading American Treaties,* p. 15. Quoted by permission of The Macmillan Company.

heritance, but is given a period of time in which to liquidate it and to remove the proceeds of such liquidation.

In several treaties provision is made whereby aliens may take possession of real property obtained by inheritance or by will.[10] For example, the treaty with New Granada (1846) provides that

> The citizens of each of the contracting parties shall have power to dispose of their personal goods or real estate within the jurisdiction of the other, by sale, donation, testament, or otherwise; and their representatives being citizens of the other party, shall succeed to their said personal goods and real estate, whether by testament or *ab intestato,* and they may take possession thereof, either by themselves or others acting for them, and dispose of the same at their will, paying such dues only as the inhabitants of the country wherein said goods are shall be subject to pay in like cases.

The whole tenor of the provision just quoted hardly justifies the opinion that it amounts to any more than the provisions discussed previously. To be sure it is stipulated that aliens "may take possession thereof." However, the rest of the article seems to indicate that its purpose is not to give aliens the right of holding the real property indefinitely. To permit them to hold indefinitely would defeat any municipal legislation which excludes aliens from taking real property by operation of law. It is difficult to see how an alien could demand absolute equality on the basis of such a provision.

Three of the treaties (Swiss Confederation, 1850; Nicaragua, 1867; San Salvador, 1870) make specific recognition of the fact that in the United States ownership of real property is determined by the state governments and not by the central government. They provide for national treatment in states permitting aliens to hold real property and for the

[10] Bavaria (1845); New Granada (1846); Salvador (1850); Two Sicilies (1855); Salvador (1870); Peru (1870); Peru (1887).

right of liquidation of inheritances in states whose legislation places limitation upon alien ownership of real property. Aliens are to receive national treatment in the inheritance of "real estate situated within the States of the American Union, or within the Republic of Salvador, in which foreigners shall be entitled to hold and inherit real estate." But if such property is situated in a state in which alienage is a bar to complete enjoyment of possession, these treaties provide that the alien heir shall be allowed a period of time in which to liquidate his inheritance and remove the proceeds.

Any investigation of the treaty provisions concerning the transmission and inheritance of real property makes it quite evident that the United States government has not entered into any treaties which *completely* deprive the states of their power to decide who shall acquire and continue in possession of real property. Treaties have interfered with the freedom of the state governments in the matter of acquiring real property, particularly those treaties subsequent to the World War. But even here there is no extension to aliens of the right to acquire any real property for any purposes they desire. It is clear, of course, that aliens have a much broader right to acquire real property under the postwar treaties than they had formerly, but even this extension falls short of complete national treatment. Under the law of most states of the United States, the alien gets much better treatment than is required by American treaty arrangements.

The treaties still leave it to the state governments to decide whether aliens may or may not continue in possession of real property acquired by inheritance. If the state government permits this, then there are treaties requiring national treatment, thereby preventing the state, at least as far as the nationals of the contracting parties are concerned, from discriminating against them. But on the other hand, if the state governments decide that aliens shall not acquire real property by inheritance, the only provision to be found in the treaties is that aliens, nationals of the other contracting party, inheriting real property in such states shall have the right not of holding the property, but merely of liquidating it and removing the proceeds. All of which seems to indicate clearly that "the Government of the United States has exhibited restraint in generally refraining from attempts to hinder the several States of the Union from shaping their own policies with regard to lands within their respective territorial limits."[11]

10. *Liberty of conscience and freedom of worship:*—In view of the treaty provisions in this matter, it is believed that nationals of one contracting party might possibly enjoy a treatment better than national treatment in the territories of the other party. It is conceivable that the states which are parties to the various treaties might enact legislation seriously infringing liberty of conscience and freedom of worship for their own nationals. Yet they are bound by an international obligation to extend to the nationals of the other party "the most perfect and entire security of conscience, without their being liable to be disturbed or molested on account of their religious belief."[12] It is true that provisions creating this possible situation are in the minority. Most of the treaties, while extending the above mentioned freedom, make the enjoyment of the grant contingent upon the fact that they must submit "to the constitution, the laws, and the established usages of the country where they reside." It was not until the latter part of the last century that the right to erect religious edifices was specifically recognized in treaty commitments. This extension of the provision made its appearance in the treaty with the Congo (1891) and appears no more until the postwar treaties, in all of which it is to be found.

[11] C. C. Hyde, *International Law*, I, 354. Quoted by permission of Little, Brown & Company.
[12] For citations to various treaties extending this protection see below, Appendix A (10).

PROVISIONS RELATIVE TO SHIPS AND GOODS

11. *Equal treatment in the matter of carrying goods:*— After the World War, the United States government perfected its commercial treaties by standardizing their provisions and bringing them up to date. Secretary of State C. E. Hughes was in a large measure responsible for this much needed improvement.[13]

Most treaties considered have provisions requiring that the contracting parties shall make no difference in their import and export charges upon those goods brought in or carried out in vessels of the other contracting party. A typical provision of this nature is that found in the fifth article of the treaty with Peru (1851):

All kinds of merchandise and articles of commerce which may be lawfully imported into the ports and territories of either of the high contracting parties in national vessels may also be so imported in vessels of the other party, without paying other or higher duties and charges of any kind or denomination whatever than if the same merchandise and articles of commerce were imported in national vessels; nor shall any distinction be made in the manner of making payment of the said duties or charges.

The seventh article of the treaty makes provision for goods exported from the countries, the specific stipulation being as follows:

All kinds of merchandise and articles of commerce which may be lawfully exported from the ports and territories of either of the high contracting parties in national vessels, may also be exported in vessels of the other party; and they shall be subject to the same duties only, and be entitled to the same drawbacks, bounties and allowances, whether the same merchandise and articles of commerce be exported in vessels of the one party or in vessels of the other.

Attention is called to the fact that the provisions quoted above do not confine national treatment of ships merely to

[13] In this connection see S. F. Bemis (ed.), *American Secretaries of State and their Diplomacy,* X, 309-317 and bibliography.

the carriage of goods between the ports of the contracting parties. No geographic limitation is placed upon the right to carry goods imported or exported. They provide for equal treatment in the matter of duties, drawbacks, and other allowances, regardless of where the arriving ship is coming from, or whither the departing ship is bound. Therefore, an agreement of this nature between two nations extends equal treatment for their ships not only to goods traveling between the ports of the two contracting parties, but also to any carrying trade between one of the contracting parties and a third country in which the vessel of the other party is engaged.

12. *The right to load and unload parts of cargo at different ports:*—The coastal trade is reserved for national vessels. However, this does not imply that a ship coming from abroad must load and unload all of its cargo at one port. Foreign vessels have the right

to discharge part of their cargoes at any port open to foreign commerce in the territory of either of the high contracting parties and to proceed with the remainder of their cargo to any other port or ports of the same territory open to foreign commerce, without paying other or higher tonnage dues or port charges in such cases than would be paid by national vessels in like circumstances and they shall be permitted to load in like manner at different ports in the same voyage outward. [Spain, 1902]

Such an arrangement as this obviously facilitates international commerce. In view of the uniform practice of this country and other maritime states such a provision does seem to be a product of overabundant caution. It is very doubtful if it is necessary in the treaties of the type into which the United States government has entered. However, nations having such a provision in their treaties are more certain of their protection against any future efforts on the part of the other party to establish a single port of entry and thereby bring into operation the host of inconveniences attendant upon any such procedure. But the possibility of any such policy seems exceedingly remote in these times.

13. *Charges upon ships as such:*—In addition to extending equality of treatment to carriage of goods and the duties and other charges placed upon such goods, the treaties extend equal treatment to vessels as such. It is customary for ports to charge ships various types of dues, such as tonnage, pilotage, and quarantine. These are charges placed upon the vessels regardless of whether or not they are carrying cargo. That is to say, they are levies independent of charges such as import duties. A typical provision extending equal treatment to ships in the matter of what may be called ship charges is to be found in the treaty with Japan of 1911. The eleventh article of this treaty stipulated:

No duties of tonnage, harbor, pilotage, lighthouse, quarantine, or other similar or corresponding duties of whatever denomination, levied in the name or for the profit of the Government, public functionaries, private individuals, corporations or establishments of any kind shall be imposed in the ports of the territories of either country upon the vessels of the other, which shall not equally, under the same conditions, be imposed on national vessels in general, or on vessels of the most favored nation. Such equality of treatment shall apply reciprocally to the respective vessels from whatever place they may arrive and whatever may be the place of destination.

14. *Prohibition of discrimination in governmental purchases of goods imported in ships of either party:*—Between 1827 (treaty with the Hanseatic Republics) and 1855 (treaty with the Two Sicilies) several of the treaties contained an article forbidding the governments of either of the contracting parties or any corporation or individual acting in their behalf to discriminate in the purchase of goods originating in the territory of the other contracting party and imported into the territory of the first party in ships of the foreign

state. However, the majority of treaties having a provision of this type do not confine the requirement of equal treatment to goods carried in national ships from the territory of one contracting party to the other. The second group of treaties has two types of grants. In the Greek treaty of 1837 it is provided:

> Each of the two high contracting parties engages not to grant in its purchases, or in those which might be made by companies or agents, acting in its name, or under its authority, any preference to importations made in its own vessels, *or in those of a third state,* over those made in the vessels of the other contracting party. [Italics mine.]

Most of the treaties of this group (Prussia, 1828; Sardinia, 1838; Hanover, 1840; Hanover, 1846; Mecklenburg-Schwerin, 1847; Two Sicilies, 1855) do not specifically prohibit discrimination between vessels of the other party and vessels of third states. Although, like the provision in the agreement with Greece, they do not limit the prohibition of discrimination only to goods, the "growth, produce or manufacture" of the other state, they are not as extensive as the Greek provision in that discrimination is not prohibited in making purchases imported in vessels of the other party and those of a third state. As an example of this type, the treaty with Prussia (1828) provides:

> No priority or preference shall be given, directly or indirectly, by either of the contracting parties, nor by any company, corporation, or agent acting on their behalf, or under their authority, in the purchase of any article of commerce, lawfully imported, on account of, or in reference to, the character of the vessel, whether it be of the one party, or of the other, in which such article was imported; it being the true intent and meaning of the contracting parties, that no distinction or any difference whatever, shall be made in this respect.

15. *Shipwreck:*—Most of the treaties contain a provision

for equal treatment in case of shipwreck. These provisions are remarkably uniform in their purposes and no substantial difference has been found in them. An example of this provision is to be found in the Spanish treaty of 1902, which stipulates that "in cases of shipwreck, damages at sea, or forced putting in, each party shall afford to the vessels of the other, whether belonging to the State or to individuals, the same assistance and protection and the same immunities which would have been granted to its own vessels in similar cases."

One writer is of the opinion that "that [type of] provision is today a relic; but during the thirteenth and fourteenth centuries, and even later kings would confiscate wrecks of foreigners that had foundered upon their shores."[14] He was referring to Article XVIII of the French treaty of 1778.

Such reasoning ignores the real purpose of articles such as these, relative to mutual assistance. They can hardly be considered as relics. The Polish treaty of 1931 has such a provision. It is suggested that the reason for the inclusion of such provision in the treaties is to prevent discrimination in salvage dues and other charges payable in this situation.

It may be said by way of conclusion that the middle of the last century marks a change in national treatment provisions as found in American treaties. When the purpose of traders in foreign countries was primarily one of importing and exporting, the treaty provisions confined themselves almost exclusively to national treatment in matters of navigation. When international intercourse became more extensive and a great increase of aliens resident in foreign countries resulted, there was an increased extension of national treatment to matters not necessarily connected with or directly a part of international commercial activity. There was oc-

[14] C. E. Hill, *op. cit.*, p. 16.

casioned a development of national treatment provisions, an evolution from mere commercial rights and privileges to practically all of the civil rights enjoyed by native citizens.

The rights and privileges enjoyed by aliens as a result of customary and conventional international law have been considered in this and the preceding chapter. In the following chapters consideration is to be given to the rights and privileges that aliens enjoy by virtue of American municipal law.

III

PROPERTY RIGHTS OF ALIENS

REAL PROPERTY

UNDER THE American system the acquisition and transmission of property is principally controlled by the state governments. The federal government, acting as a local or state government, performs a similar function in the territories. Hence one is able to arrive at a true appraisal of the alien's rights relative to real property only by a study of state legislation. It is proposed here to investigate the status of aliens as declared by the several state governments, and to attempt some conclusions as to the extent of national treatment accorded aliens in this matter.

It is necessary to set forth a brief summary of the common law rules, and then to ascertain to what extent these have been modified by state legislation.

Under the common law an alien could acquire land by purchase but not by descent; that is to say, he could be a devisee but not an heir. His title to such acquisition was good as against anyone but the state.[1] In other words, the alien could hold land until a forfeiture in favor of the state was enforced by a proceeding of "office found." However, the state could not arbitrarily assume that a person was an alien and then proceed to take his real property. Alienage had definitely to be established by the proceeding before the

---

[1] *Fairfax's Devisee v. Hunter's Lessee* (1813), 7 Cranch 603; *Governeur's Heirs v. Robertson* (1826), 11 Wheat. 332; *Orr v. Hodgson* (1819), 4 Wheat. 453; *Phillips v. Moore* (1879), 100 U. S. 208.

property escheated to the state, and before the state acquired a valid title therein.[2]

The common law allowed an alien to devise his property to citizens or to other aliens. However, the property of an alien dying intestate did not descend to his heirs if they were also aliens. The theory of this was that the alien had no heritable blood. On the same theory an alien could not claim land from a citizen if the relationship could be traced only through an alien.[3]

1. *State legislation relative to aliens' rights:*—Legislation enacted from time to time by the several states has done much to modify the common law. Likewise, the federal government, through the exercise of its treaty-making power, has in turn modified and liberalized some of the state legislation which operates as a limitation upon the alien's right to acquire and transmit real property upon a basis equal to that enjoyed by citizens of the United States.

In most of the states of the United States the common law disability has been removed.[4] Thirty-five states permit all aliens to take property by descent. In some of these states, however, there are statutes which discriminate against certain classes of aliens in the matter of *continuing to hold that real property* which they have acquired by descent. Fourteen states,[5] while removing the common law disability of aliens to acquire and to pass real property by descent, have statutes which permit an alien's continuing in possession of such property only if he meets certain legal requirements as indicated in Appendix B, Table 4, below; that is, friendly aliens, bona fide residents, declarants, and others.

Of the remaining states, seven permit only aliens who are eligible to citizenship under the laws of the United States

[2] *Fairfax's Devisee v. Hunter's Lessee.*
[3] H. T. Tiffany, *The Law of Real Property*, III, 2350-2352.
[4] See below, Appendix B, Table 4.
[5] Georgia, Illinois, Indiana, Iowa, Kentucky, Maryland, Montana, Nevada, New York, Oklahoma, Texas, Vermont, Virginia, and Washington.

to acquire real property by descent.[6] Six states permit only aliens who are residents or declarants to acquire real property by descent.[7]

As pointed out above, the common law permitted aliens to acquire real property by purchase. The title to real property so acquired was good as against everyone except the state. Many states through legislation have deprived themselves of the common law right to take real property owned by aliens through an "office found" proceeding. In other words they have extended to the alien national treatment in the matter of acquiring real property by purchase.[8]

Twenty-seven states permit all aliens to acquire real property by purchase. However, fifteen of these place limitations upon the length of time an alien may hold property and the amount of property he may so acquire.

Some states have enacted legislation which effects a contraction of an alien's rights under the common law. They either grant the right to acquire real property by purchase only to persons eligible to citizenship under the laws of the United States,[9] or only to persons who either have declared their intention to become citizens or are residents of the state.[10]

It may be said that so far as resident aliens are concerned they receive national treatment in the acquisition of real property in thirty states.[11] Resident aliens receive national treatment in the acquisition of real property by descent in thirty-five states.[12] In other words, in thirty states resident aliens receive national treatment in the acquisition of real property by purchase as well as by descent, while in five

[6] See below, Appendix B, Table 5.   [7] Ibid., Table 6.
[8] Ibid., Table 1.   [9] Ibid., Table 2.   [10] Ibid., Table 3.
[11] Alabama, Arkansas, Colorado, Connecticut, Delaware, Georgia, Iowa, Maine, Maryland, Massachusetts, Michigan, Minnesota, Mississippi, New Hampshire, New Jersey, New York, North Carolina, North Dakota, Ohio, Oklahoma, Rhode Island, South Dakota, Tennessee, Texas, Utah, Vermont, Virginia, West Virginia, Wisconsin, Wyoming.
[12] Alabama, Arkansas, Colorado, Connecticut, Delaware, Florida, Georgia, Iowa, Maine, Maryland, Massachusetts, Michigan, Minnesota, Mississippi, Mis-

other states[13] the law affords national treatment in inheritance but offers less than national treatment in the acquisition by purchase.

2. *Treaty provisions relative to the acquisition of real property by aliens:*—The United States government has entered into many international agreements containing provisions relative to the alien's rights to real property. In addition to the modifications of common law disabilities to be found in legislation of the several states, aliens also have treaty guaranties of the same nature. It is believed, however, that the alien obtains greater rights with respect to the acquisition and disposal of real property in the United States from state legislation. The treaty provisions, as a whole, are less extensive than state laws upon the matter.

As shown above, one of the major disabilities of an alien at common law was that he possessed no heritable blood. Hence, if he died in intestacy leaving only alien heirs, the law prescribing the descent of such property to his relatives did not operate in his case because of his alienage and the alienage of his heirs. Provisions in the American treaties relating to the possession of real property by aliens may be classified in two major categories, those concerned with the alien's right to obtain real property *ab intestato* and those dealing with acquisition of real property by purchase.

By far the majority of provisions deal with the first of these two groups.[14] A typical example of such provision is Article XI of the Spanish treaty of 1795:

And where, on the death of any person holding real estate within the territories of the one party, such real estate would by the laws of the land descend on a citizen or subject of the other, were he not disqualified by being an alien, such subject

---

souri, Nebraska, New Hampshire, New Jersey, New York, North Carolina, North Dakota, Ohio, Oklahoma, Pennsylvania, Rhode Island, South Carolina, South Dakota, Tennessee, Texas, Utah, Vermont, Virginia, West Virginia, Wisconsin, Wyoming.

[13] Florida, Missouri, Nebraska, Pennsylvania, South Carolina.

[14] See below, Appendix B, Table 8.

shall be allowed a reasonable time to sell the same, and to withdraw the proceeds without molestation, and exempt from all rights of detraction on the part of the government of the respective states.[15]

As far as the United States is concerned, the purpose of the provision is to remove the common law disability placed upon aliens to succeed *ab intestato* to real property. An alien, citizen or subject of a country having such treaty arrangement with the United States, is protected against any return to the common law which states may make. It is true that thirty-five states have removed this common law disability by legislation;[16] however, the treaty provisions function as a guarantee against any reversal of legislative policy on the part of state governments.

Treaty provisions relative to aliens' acquisition of real property by descent do not in most instances permit aliens to receive property upon the same basis as citizens. For the most part, the state governments determine one's right to real property and prescribe the manner in which such property is to be enjoyed in the United States.[17] It is a principle of American constitutional law that a treaty takes precedence over a conflicting state constitution or legislation. However, the federal government has used the treaty-making power in this connection cautiously. Most of the provisions do not give the alien the right to obtain real property *ab intestato* in the fullest sense. What these provisions do grant is the right to dispose of the real property inherited and to remove the proceeds of such disposal. This arrangement assures to the alien the market value of the property and leaves the state governments free to keep the real estate situated in their jurisdictions out of alien hands should they so desire. The provisions[18] do not deny the state the power to determine who shall own real property within

[15] 8 *Stat.* 144.   [16] See below, Appendix B, Table 4.
[17] *U. S. v. Fox* (1876), 94 U. S. 315.
[18] See below, Appendix B, Table 8 (a).

its jurisdiction. In fact they specifically recognize this power by the phrase, "were he not disqualified by being an alien." Therefore, in most of the provisions concerned with descent of real property to aliens, all that is granted is that when "such real estate would by the laws of the land [in the United States this means state laws] descend on a citizen or subject of the other, such citizen or subject shall be allowed," not to enter into full and complete enjoyment and possession thereof, but to have a specified time or a reasonable time "to sell the same and to withdraw the proceeds." The treaty-making power has been used to modify the common law to the benefit of alien heirs. By virtue of these provisions, aliens have been extended national treatment in that they receive distributive shares in cases of intestacy the same as citizens. They further grant aliens the right to sell that which they obtain by operation of law. But here the provisions stop. They do not grant aliens the right to enter into unconditional possession.

Another group of provisions,[19] much smaller than the one considered immediately above, is composed of provisions which do not specify that disposal must be made within a reasonable time or a specified time. They merely provide that aliens may inherit real property and dispose of it "at their will."

A third group[20] stipulates that aliens may obtain real property *ab intestato* "without being obliged to obtain letters of naturalization." No mention is made of the necessity of disposing of such inheritance. In interpreting the provision of one of these treaties, the United States Supreme Court said that "the direct object of this stipulation is to give French subjects the rights of citizens so far as respects property. . . . It does away with the incapacity of alienage and places the defendants in error in precisely the same situation, with respect to lands, as if they had become citizens."[21]

---

[19] *Ibid.*, (b).   [20] *Ibid.*, (c).
[21] *Chirac v. Chirac* (1817), 2 Wheat. 259.

Hence, it seems that this small group of provisions goes much further than the others in removing alien incapacity to inherit real property in the United States. There is also to be found in American treaties a type of provision which defines an alien's right to acquire real property through his own initiative;[22] that is to say, to acquire such property by means other than receiving it by testament or *ab intestato*. As can be seen from the table just cited, most of these provisions are concerned only with buildings, and very few of the provisions make any mention of the alien's rights in land as such. Furthermore, it is to be noticed that the alien is quite limited as to the manner in which he may make use of buildings. He has rights only in connection with those necessary for residential and commercial purposes. Moreover, in many of the treaties the alien is further limited in that he may only "rent and occupy" or "hire and occupy" buildings and not own them. In short, most of the treaty provisions do not grant the privilege of acquisition and use of buildings in as full a manner as is enjoyed by nationals.

Aliens' rights in connection with land as such are considered in very few of the treaty provisions. In most of the provisions in which land is considered, the alien is granted merely the right to lease land. Moreover, there is a further limitation in that it is to be leased for commercial or residential purposes. This, of course, means that land may not be obtained for agricultural purposes.[23] In recent years there has been some widening of this privilege in that the treaties subsequent to the Siamese treaty of 1920 have permitted the leasing of lands for religious, charitable, and mortuary, as well as for commercial and residential, purposes. In only five of the treaties considered in this connection can it be said that an alien obtains treatment fully equal to that accorded nationals in the matter of acquiring and using land.[24]

[22] See below, Appendix B, Table 9.
[23] See *Porterfield v. Webb* (1923), 263 U. S. 225.
[24] See below, Appendix B, Table 10.

3. *Court interpretation of treaty provisions:*—The treaty provisions discussed above were divided into two general classifications, those concerned with acquisition by action of the alien himself, and those concerned with acquisition by inheritance from others. The cases interpreting these two general types of provisions are now to be considered in this order.

A series of cases has resulted from the antialien land laws enacted by the legislatures of several states. These statutes provided in substance that aliens, ineligible for citizenship under the laws of the United States, were barred from acquiring land within their jurisdictions for agricultural purposes. The cases, with two exceptions, involve attempts made by subjects of Japan to acquire land for agricultural purposes.

In the cases involving Japanese subjects, the attempt was made to prove that the state statutes were repugnant to the treaty between the United States and Japan of 1911.[25] Article I provides that "the citizens or subjects of each of the High Contracting Parties shall have liberty . . . to lease land for residential and commercial purposes . . . upon the same terms as native citizens or subjects."

In the case of *Terrace v. Thompson,* the United States Supreme Court said:

We think that the treaty not only contains no provision giving Japanese the right to own or lease land for agricultural purposes, but, when viewed in the light of the negotiations leading up to its consummation, the language shows that the high contracting parties respectively intended to withhold a treaty grant of that right to the citizens or subjects of either in the territories of the other. The right to "carry on trade" or "to own or lease and occupy houses" . . . cannot be said to include the right to own or lease or have any title or interest in land for agricultural purposes.[26]

[25] 37 *Stat.* 1504.
[26] (1923), 263 U. S. 197. See also *Porterfield v. Webb.*

This involved the land law of the state of Washington. A year before, the California court had made the same interpretation.[27]

The treaty with Japan does not give Japanese subjects the right to lease land; nor does it give them the right to any indirect benefits from lands used for agricultural purposes. An attempt was made in California, not to lease land, but to enter into a cropping contract. Again the United States Supreme Court upheld the state statute on the grounds that "the privilege to make and carry out the proposed cropping contract, or to have the right to the possession, enjoyment and benefit of land for agricultural purposes as contemplated and provided for [in the cropping contract] is not given to Japanese subjects by the treaty."[28]

When a Japanese subject made an attempt to buy shares of stock in a farming company, the United States Supreme Court upheld the state's interference upon the ground that the state "may forbid indirect as well as direct ownership and control of agricultural land by ineligible aliens. The right 'to carry on trade' given by the treaty does not give the privilege to acquire the stock above described."[29]

Subjects of the British Empire have also attempted unsuccessfully to obtain agricultural lands in violation of these state statutes. The Washington statute provides as a condition precedent to acquisition or the enjoyment of the benefits of agricultural land that the alien must have declared his intention to become naturalized. O'Connell, a British subject, had not so declared his intention, but had attempted to enter into a situation where he would be benefited by profits from agricultural lands located in the state of Washington. He pleaded, in substance, that money produced by land was not real property but was personalty and the state could not

[27] *Ex parte Y. Akado* (1922), 207 Pac. (Cal.) 245. See also *Ex parte Okahara* (1923), 216 Pac. (Cal.) 614.

[28] *Webb v. O'Brien* (1923), 263 U. S. 313.

[29] *Frick v. Webb* (1923), 263 U. S. 326.

arbitrarily "convert what is commonly and universally recognized as personal property into real estate or an interest therein, and thereby cause an escheat." Then, after maintaining that what he would receive from the land was in legal contemplation personalty, he pleaded Article II of the British treaty of 1899,[30] which protects British subjects in the possession of personalty. But the Washington court found his reasoning faulty. The court held:

> It may be admitted that the Legislature may not by mere arbitrary definition convert that which has always been known as personal property into real property, because such legislation would be in violation of the spirit of the treaty. But there are certain things which, in and by themselves, would be considered personal property, yet, because of their close and intimate connection with the land, may rightly be declared to be parts of, or interests in, the land. Such are rents, issues and profits derived from land where ownership or beneficial interest therein is prohibited as by the legislation under consideration.[31]

In the case of *Carter v. Utley*[32] an Asiatic Indian, an ineligible alien, sought to enter into a contract whereby he would receive benefit from agricultural lands in California. The court could not find that he was "guaranteed this right by treaty or otherwise."

Although not germane to a discussion of judicial interpretation of treaty provisions, the fate of the Arkansas anti-alien land law is of some interest at this point. The state of Arkansas passed a typical alien land law[33] which was annulled by the court of that state. The statute was attacked in the case of *Applegate v. Luke*[34] on the ground that it was repugnant to the Arkansas Constitution. Article II, section 20, of that constitution provides that "no distinction shall

[30] 31 *Stat.* 1939.
[31] *State v. O'Connell* (1922), 209 Pac. (Wash.) 865.
[32] (1924), 231 Pac. (Cal.) 559.
[33] *Arkansas, Acts 45th Gen'l. Assembly, 1925,* Act 249.
[34] (1927), 173 Ark. 93.

ever be made by the law between resident aliens and citizens in regard to the possession, enjoyment or descent of property." In view of this provision, the court was of the opinion that all resident aliens, whether eligible to naturalization under the laws of the United States or not, had the same right "to acquire and enjoy the possession of property . . . that any natural citizen has."

An example of the second type of provision having to do with acquisition of land is to be found in the French treaty of 1853. In this treaty it is provided that "in all of the States of the Union, *whose existing laws permit it* . . . Frenchmen shall enjoy the right of possessing . . . real property by the same title and in the same manner as the citizens of the United States."[35]

In a Tennessee case[36] there was a dispute as to the right of a Frenchman to deed property to another, and, because it involved a deeding of property, it was contended that the French treaty did not apply. The Tennessee Supreme Court thought otherwise. The court pointed out that at the time of the execution of the deed "the State of Tennessee was one of the States of the Union 'by whose existing laws aliens were permitted to hold real estate' on the terms prescribed in its own enactment; and hence the treaty of 1853 has a direct application. . . ." Construing the law in connection with the treaty, the court had "no hesitation in holding that as to the subjects of France, they are invested by the law and the treaty together with the right to make an indefeasible title by deed or otherwise, of lands owned by them in this state." It follows therefore, that if the laws of the state permit Frenchmen to own real property, the treaty guarantees them the right to handle that property in any manner that the laws of the particular state of the Union permit to citizens of that state.

[35] 10 *Stat.* 996, Art. VII. Italics mine.
[36] *Baker v. Shy* (1871), 9 Heiskell (Tenn.) 85.

A Louisiana law provided that any inheritance of property owned in and by a person residing in Louisiana by a nonresident alien was subject to a tax. In the case of *Prevost v. Greneaux* a nonresident French heir protested payment of the tax on the ground that his liability to such payment was removed by the treaty of 1853 with France. The case went to the United States Supreme Court.[37] Here the tribunal is brought absolutely face to face with the question of a state whose "existing laws" do not give the same benefits to aliens as to citizens. In answer the court said, "the treaty does not claim for the United States the right of controlling the succession of real or personal property in a State. . . . And as there is no act of the legislature of Louisiana repealing this law and accepting the provisions of the treaty, so as to secure to her citizens similar rights in France; this court might feel some difficulty in saying that it was repealed by this treaty, if the State court had not so expounded its own law and held Louisiana was one of the States in which the proposed arrangements of the treaty were to be carried into effect."

In another federal court case there was a suit between two heirs, one a citizen of the United States and the other a nonresident Frenchman.[38] The state law permitted aliens to hold real property. But how did this affect holdings passing to nonresident aliens? The court decided that "the provisions of the treaty apply to all states by whose laws an alien whether designated as resident or nonresident, is permitted to hold real estate. In such states, where a resident alien is permitted to hold real estate, the prohibition as to nonresidents holding title to real estate by inheritance or otherwise is inoperative, by virtue of the treaty, as to citizens of the republic of France."

---

[37] (1856), 19 How. 1.
[38] *Bahuaud v. Bize* (1901), 105 Fed. 485.

Most of the litigation in connection with treaty provisions relative to alien inheritance of real property has arisen out of controversies concerning the type of provision stipulating that when a person in the United States dies, seized of real property, and his heirs, were they not aliens, could inherit under the *lex loci rei sitae,* these alien heirs shall be given a certain time in which to liquidate the estate and remove the proceeds from the country without molestation and free from any other or greater charges than are placed upon citizens of the United States in like circumstances.

Before entering upon a discussion of the court's interpretation of these provisions it seems necessary to give a passing attention to terminological difficulties that the court has had to meet. Americans have created meanings for the words "state" and "territory" which are different from the traditional connotation of those words and have, thereby, given rise to some dispute as to their meaning in treaties.

The French treaty of 1853 stipulates that "in all States of the Union" certain things must happen. When a Frenchman brought suit for rights gained under that treaty, the other party tried to maintain that the use of the word "state" deprived the Frenchman of his rights to land in the District of Columbia. This was denied by the United States Supreme Court. It was the opinion of the court that "the District of Columbia, under the government of the United States, is as much a State as any of those political communities which compose the United States."[39]

The British treaty of 1899 provides that British subjects shall be able to succeed to property "in the territories" of the United States. In a Wyoming case it was contended that "territories of one of the contracting parties" meant territory of the United States in contradistinction to any of the

[39] *Geofroy v. Riggs* (1890), 133 U. S. 258.

states.[40] Here again the court could not agree with such reasoning.

There is some difference of judicial opinion as to the nature of the rights of aliens to real property *during* the prescribed period for liquidation of such property. During this period and before actual liquidation, do aliens have the right to enjoyment and benefit from the real property, or is their right only to sell it and remove the proceeds?

The opinion that aliens have during the prescribed period more than the mere right to sell is best illustrated in the New York case of *Kull v. Kull*.[41] The court said:

> We think there is no reason to doubt but that under the provisions of the treaty the alien heir may come to the State and at once enter into possession, use and enjoyment of the property, and exercise all the rights of ownership and advantages of possession for the purpose of making the sale, because these rights are manifestly intended by the treaty to be conferred upon him. In short, in our judgment the treaty intends to confer on the alien heir, for the period of two years, precisely the same rights he would enjoy if he were a resident alien, imposing upon him simply the obligation to sell and convey the fee to some other party capable of holding within that period. . . . Meanwhile, he may possess and take care of the property, improve it and exercise all the authority of owner, for the purpose of making it more productive and valuable, and may himself enjoy such rents and profits as he can obtain.

It has likewise been established in the jurisdictions of Illinois,[42] Iowa,[43] Nebraska,[44] and Wyoming[45] that the right to sell and remove the proceeds of sale also includes the alien's right to the enjoyment of all the benefits of ownership until such sale is made or until the termination

[40] *Bamforth v. Ihmsen* (1922), 204 Pac. (Wyo.) 345.
[41] (1885), 37 Hun (N. Y.) 476.
[42] *Schultze v. Schultze* (1893), 33 N. E. (Ill.) 201.
[43] *Ahrens v. Ahrens* (1909), 123 N. W. (Iowa) 164.
[44] *Pierson v. Lawler* (1917), 161 N. W. (Neb.) 419.
[45] *Bamforth v. Ihmsen.*

of the period allowed by law for the liquidation of the property.

In 1883, two years before the *Kull* case, a New York court had held just the opposite. At that time, the New York court said that the treaty "does not by implication give the title to the alien, as the title is not requisite to the power of sale which can exist and be executed without it. . . . And it is clearly implied from the language used in article four [treaty with Hesse, 1844][46] that while an alien may own the personal property, he has simply a power of sale as to the real property."[47]

In a California case[48] it was contended that the right to sell was "a mere empty privilege, worthless without its being coupled with the right of possession." But the court differed with this contention on the grounds that, "the laws of this State expressly authorize sales of real estate by parties out of possession, so then the party may freely exercise the privileges guaranteed by the treaty [Hanseatic Republics, 1827]."[49]

Many of the provisions prescribing a definite period for liquidation have an additional phrase to the effect that the prescribed period may be "reasonably prolonged." It is for the courts to determine the reasonableness of any prolongation and also the validity of the circumstances necessitating it.

In an Illinois case, it was contended that alien heirs must take some definite steps to secure a prolongation of the period and that such time could be prolonged only by an act of the same department of the government which consummated the treaty and thereby established the limitation.[50] It seems that this was the first time such a contention was made. The court admits in the opinion that it can find no

---

[46] 9 *Stat.* 819.
[47] *Bollermann v. Blake* (1883), 94 N. Y. 624.
[48] *Siemssen v. Bofer* (1856), 6 Cal. 250. [49] 8 *Stat.* 370.
[50] *Scharpf v. Schmidt* (1898), 50 N. E. (Ill.) 182.

precedent for its decision. After considering the facts, and starting from the premise that the "construction of treaties is the peculiar province of the judiciary when a case arises between individuals," the court held that the phrase "may be reasonably prolonged" meant that the court would decide upon the set of facts peculiar to each case if the circumstances permitted the prolongation and no specific application for prolongation was necessary.

Fifteen years earlier the New York court had intimated in an obiter dictum that such should be the law when in an opinion it said: "It is possible that what would be a reasonable prolongation of the term might upon the facts appearing in any case be a judicial question for the determination of the courts."[51] The finding of law on this point in the *Scharpf* case has been approved by the highest courts of Nebraska[52] and Wyoming.[53]

Several treaties provide that "goods and effects" are to be inheritable. Actions have arisen under this provision where aliens have pleaded that the term "goods and effects" includes real property. As to whether this is true, there is a difference of opinion. Early in the last century it was held in the case of the *University v. Miller*[54] that "effects descending by inheritance must include land," because "unless the meaning of the word be extended to things immovable, nothing at all is granted by the word 'effects'; for by our law alienage is no objection to the acquisition of movables in any way, either by purchase or by succession *ab intestato*." The same interpretation was made sixty-six years later in Illinois[55] and seventy-nine years later in Washington.[56]

The contrary position has been held in Iowa and Kansas jurisdictions. In *Meier v. Lee*[57] the Iowa court was "of the

[51] *Bollermann v. Blake.*
[52] *Pierson v. Lawler; Fischer v. Sklenar* (1917), 163 N. W. (Neb.) 861.
[53] *Bamforth v. Ihmsen.*   [54] (1831), 14 N. C. (3 Dev.) 188.
[55] *Adams v. Akerlund* (1897), 48 N. E. (Ill.) 454.
[56] *In re Stixrud's Estate* (1910), 109 Pac. (Wash.) 343.
[57] (1898), 76 N. W. (Iowa) 712.

opinion that it [Swedish treaty of 1827 which revived Article VI of the treaty of 1783][58] does not apply to lands." With approval, the Kansas court said: "We are inclined to agree with the Supreme Court of Iowa and hold that the words 'goods and effects' as used . . . do not mean or embrace real estate."[59]

4. *Summary:*—The major disability of aliens under the common law was that they could not acquire real property by operation of law; that is to say, the law for the distribution of property in cases of intestacy did not operate for aliens. In many of the states this disability has been removed and aliens may take by succession as well as by devise. A few states have enacted legislation which has modified the common law in another manner. These so-called antialien land laws not only limit the classes of aliens who may take by descent but also by purchase. However, the great majority of states extend national treatment to aliens in the acquisition of real property.

The treaties into which the United States government has entered which contain provisions relative to acquisition of real property by aliens are by no means as liberal as state legislation in this matter. Most of the provisions to be found are concerned with removing the common law disability to take by descent. However, in most instances, this is limited to the right to liquidate the property and remove the proceeds without molestation. Many provisions give aliens the right to take by purchase, but limit this right to property necessary primarily for commercial and residential purposes. In a remarkably few treaties is there to be found that which can actually be termed complete national treatment. Therefore, the alien obtains in the United States as a whole infinitely more liberal treatment as a result of state legislation than as a result of treaty commitments.

[58] Treaty of 1827, 8 *Stat.* 346; Treaty of 1783, 8 *Stat.* 60.
[59] *Johnson v. Olson* (1914), 142 Pac. (Kan.) 256.

COPYRIGHTS, PATENTS, TRADE-MARKS

According to American law copyrights, patents, and trade-marks are considered personal property. In explanation of aliens' rights and privileges in these three types of possessions, an attempt will be made to demonstrate the fact that under American municipal law aliens virtually receive national treatment, and that they are as amply protected in their enjoyment of such possessions as they could be by treaty provisions.

1. *Copyright:*—At common law an author's property in his unpublished work is considered as any other property and the judicial remedies for the protection of other property are applicable to the protection of property of this nature. However, the rights of authors run only to publication, and thereafter their sole protection is under copyright statutes. In the United States an author has no exclusive property in a published work except such as is .extended by congressional enactment of copyright statutes.[60] The purpose of the copyright is to overcome the common law disability whereby as soon as one published his work it became public property and the producer lost his property in the thing published. By virtue of copyright legislation, the benefits resulting from literary production are exclusively reserved to the author for a period of years.

Article I, section 8, of the United States Constitution gives Congress the power to promote and foster literary achievement by means of copyright legislation. It is suggested, however, that the right to a copyright is not inherently a constitutional right. Due to constitutional phraseology, the means of securing this right are to be prescribed by congressional action. In short, to quote Mr. Justice Blatchford: "No authority exists for obtaining a copyright beyond the extent to which Congress has authorized it. A copyright cannot be sustained as a right existing at common law; but,

[60] *Wheaton v. Peters* (1832), Fed. Cas. 17,486.

as it exists in the United States, it depends *wholly* on the legislation of Congress."[61]

The earliest congressional legislation relative to copyright in the United States was the Act of May 31, 1790.[62] This statute made no discrimination between alien and national when providing in its first section that the benefits of copyright were to be extended to any person or persons "being a citizen or citizens thereof [United States], or resident within the same." Since that date no distinction has been made between citizens and *resident* aliens.

The only discrimination against aliens in American copyright legislation down to the Act of March 3, 1891,[63] was that in all acts anterior to the Act of 1891 there is to be found a provision similar to the following: "That nothing in this act shall be construed to extend to prohibit the importation or vending, reprinting, or publishing within the United States, of any map, chart, book or books, written, printed, or published by any person not a citizen of the United States, in foreign parts or places without the jurisdiction of the United States."[64]

From the very beginning of the government under the Constitution resident aliens have been treated as nationals in matters relating to copyrighting their intellectual productions. The only requirement made in addition to those imposed upon nationals was the requirement of residence. Even this has received liberal interpretation. The courts have held that the residence of aliens was a matter of intention and that compliance with the residence requirement did not depend upon any period or measurement of time. Judge Drummond, in his charge to the jury, interpreted this requirement:

In order to constitute residence, it is necessary that a man should go to a place and take up his abode there with the in-

---

[61] *Banks v. Manchester* (1888), 128 U. S. 244. Italics mine.
[62] 1 *Stat.* 124.   [63] 26 *Stat.* 1106.   [64] Act of 1790, sec. 5.

tention of remaining, making it his home. If he does that, then he is a resident of that place. This question of residence is not to be determined by the length of time that the person may remain in a particular place. . . . A man may go into a place and take up his abode there with the intention of remaining, and if so, he becomes a resident there, although he may afterwards change his mind, and within a short time remove.[65]

The filing of a declaration of intention to become a citizen of the United States did not give an alien the residence necessary for the enjoyment of copyright privileges in this country. The test of residence was intention in the case of *Carey v. Collier*. A British naval officer's oath of intention to become a citizen was not acceptable as a proof of intentional residence after the court had considered the evidence brought out in the case. The court would not be governed merely by the initiation of the naturalization process. To the court "it was evident that a man who was a mere transient visitant, whose family, business, intentions and relations were all abroad, could not be considered a resident, and the filing of a declaration of intention to become a citizen, could not make him one."[66]

Down to the Act of March 3, 1891, there can be no doubt that in the application of the common law and statutory law relative to copyright, no distinction was ever made between nationals and resident friendly aliens. It has ever been true in the United States that if, at the time the copyright is initiated, the applicant is a resident within the jurisdiction of the United States, he has merely to fulfill the statutory requirements which are sufficient to support an application by a national.

Likewise, there can be no doubt of the fact that it was the intention of the United States government from the Act of 1790 to the Act of 1891 to confine the benefits of

---

[65] *Boucicault v. Wood* (1867), Fed. Cas. 1,693.
[66] (*ca.* 1839), Fed. Cas. 2,400.

its copyright protection to citizens and resident aliens. Not only have these acts specifically excluded literary productions made in foreign parts and places,[67] but courts have held that legislation protected only literary productions of citizens and resident aliens and did not extend protection to productions of nonresident aliens, even though these latter assigned their work to a resident alien or citizen of the United States. Until 1891 protection could "apply only to authors who, if not citizens, must be residents of the United States, and proprietors under derivations of title from such authors. No other proprietors can obtain a copyright."[68]

The Act of March 3, 1891[69] inaugurated a more liberal policy in the treatment of aliens. The residence requirement was completely removed and has been absent from every subsequent act. Beginning with the Act of 1891 the United States government has offered copyright protection to any author. However, if one is neither a citizen of the United States nor a resident alien, a condition must be fulfilled before he is able to obtain copyright protection. It is provided that the protection granted

. . . shall only apply to a citizen or subject of a foreign state or nation when such foreign state or nation permits to citizens of the United States of America the benefit of copyright on substantially the same basis as its own citizens; or when such foreign state or nation is a party to an international agreement which provides for reciprocity in the granting of copyright, by the terms of which agreement the United States of America may, at its pleasure, become a party to such agreement. The existence of either of the conditions aforesaid shall be determined by the President of the United States by proclamation made from time to time as the purposes of this act may require.[70]

Therefore, since 1891 an alien, if not a resident, may receive copyright protection in the United States commen-

[67] See above, p. 63.
[68] *Keene v. Wheatley* (1861), Fed. Cas. 7,644. See also *Yuengling v. Schile* (1882), 12 Fed. 97.   [69] 26 *Stat.* 1106.   [70] *Ibid.,* sec. 13.

surate with that extended to nationals as soon as the President has proclaimed the fact that citizens of the United States are entitled to copyright protection in the country of the nonresident alien applicant upon substantially the same basis as the nationals of that foreign country. Not only does the President determine and proclaim the existence of equal treatment for Americans abroad, but the courts have held that it is not within their power to go behind the presidential proclamation to determine whether equal treatment was a fact at the time of the proclamation, or continued to be a fact after the proclamation.

In one case the plea was made that, although there might have been equality of treatment for Americans in Great Britain when President Taft issued his proclamation, the British government had, subsequent to the proclamation, changed the British copyright law so that it operated with inequality. To this the court replied:

> The proclamation is conclusive evidence of the fact that Great Britain at that date gave our citizens the benefit of her copyright laws on substantially the same basis as to her own citizens, and the courts have no right to review it. Since that time Great Britain has made changes in her own law which the defendants say result in a denial to our citizens of substantially the same rights as her own citizens enjoy, and insist that the court should determine this question and act accordingly. Congress, in our opinion, has confided the whole subject to the Executive exclusively. The President is required, by proclamation, to determine from time to time, as the purposes of the act may require, the existence of these reciprocal conditions. As no proclamation has been made since that of April 9, 1910, we are bound to presume that in the opinion of the Executive these conditions do still exist.[71]

The Supreme Court of the United States looks upon the presidential proclamation as "a condition of the right" to

[71] *Chappell & Co. v. Fields* (1914), 210 Fed. 864.

enjoy copyright protection in the United States if the applicant is not a resident alien.[72]

The United States government has been very liberal in extending copyright protection to literary productions of aliens. In the application of the common law no distinction is made between citizen and alien. The common law considers one's literary production a property right which is subject to the same protection as any other property until such production is published. Publication terminates the property right. However, when it is purely a matter of protecting unpublished works, the courts have been quite in agreement that no distinction shall be made between citizen and alien. For example, Judge Allen of the New York Court of Appeals has said:

> The courts of the state are open to an alien friend pursuing his property and seeking to recover it from a wrong-doer; and there is nothing in any positive law, or in the policy of the government, which would close the door against the same alien friend seeking protection for the fruits of his mental labor, by restraining its publication against his wishes. The protection afforded by the common law to literary labor is very slight at the best, but as it is, it is accorded to alien friend and citizen alike, and both are regarded with equal favor.[73]

As has been said above, the purpose of copyright statutes is to overcome the common law provision that protection does not extend after publication. In short, a copyright has for its purpose the continuation of an exclusive property right in one's literary production after publication.

The United States government has never made any distinction between citizens and resident aliens in its copyright protection. Moreover, since 1891, it has been the policy of the government to extend treatment substantially equal to

---

[72] *Bong v. Alfred S. Campbell Art Co.* (1909), 214 U. S. 236.
[73] *Palmer v. DeWitt* (1872), 47 N. Y. 532.

that given its nationals to those nonresident aliens whose governments extend equality of treatment to Americans.

2. *Patents:*—In patent legislation the United States government has not been so consistently nondiscriminatory as in copyright legislation. For a short period letters patent could be obtained only by citizens, which situation never existed in connection with copyright.

The earliest patent statute was enacted in 1790. The first section of the act provided, "that upon the petition *of any person or persons*" to the prescribed officers of the United States, if the said officers "shall deem the invention or discovery sufficiently useful and important" they shall "cause letters patent to be made out in the name of the United States . . . granting to such petitioner or petitioners, his, her, or their administrators or assigns for any term not exceeding fourteen years, the sole and exclusive right and liberty of making, constructing, using and vending to others to be used, the said invention or discovery. . . ."[74]

This liberal grant was withdrawn three years later. The Act of February 21, 1793[75] repealed the Act of 1790 and confined the right to secure patents to citizens only. Section one of the Act of 1793 provided "that when any person or persons, being a citizen or citizens of the United States," shall petition the Secretary of State for a letter patent, the Secretary shall issue the same.

This complete exclusion of aliens from patent privileges in the United States did not continue in force long. Seven years later an act was passed which provided:

That all and singular the rights and privileges given, intended, or provided to citizens of the United States respecting patents for new inventions, discoveries and improvements, by the act [of 1793] shall be, and hereby are extended and given to all aliens who at the time of petitioning in the manner prescribed by the said act, shall have resided for two years within the

---

[74] 1 *Stat.* 109. Italics mine.   [75] 1 *Stat.* 318.

United States, which privileges shall be obtained, used, and enjoyed, by such persons, in as full and ample manner, and under the same conditions, limitations and restrictions, as by the said act is provided and directed in the case of citizens of the United States . . .[76]

In applying the law concerning the privileges and limitations given to and placed upon citizens by the Act of 1793 and extended to all aliens having a two years' residence in the United States by the Act of 1800, the United States Supreme Court was of the opinion that "there can be no difference between a citizen and an alien," and under these two acts, the rights of each "must be tested by the same rule."[77]

Congress enacted its most extensive patent legislation in 1836.[78] This act repealed all former legislation and served for many years as what might be termed the patent code. This act did not put the treatment of citizens and *any* aliens upon an equal basis. It contained differences of treatment as to citizens, resident, and nonresident aliens. All three groups were entitled to petition for and receive patents for their inventions and discoveries, but differences of treatment arose as to the privileges each received in taking out a patent.

In the first place, a patentee, if an alien at the time his patent was granted, had "to put and continue on sale to the public, on reasonable terms," the invention or discovery for which the patent was issued within eighteen months after the date of such issuance.[79] Under this provision "it is not necessary . . . for an alien patentee to prove that he hawked the patented invention to obtain a market for it, or that he endeavored to sell to any person. . . . But it rests on those who seek to defeat the patent [of an alien], to prove that the patentee neglected or refused to sell the patented invention for reasonable prices when application was

[76] Act of 1800, 2 *Stat.* 37, sec. 1.   [77] *Shaw v. Cooper* (1833), 7 Pet. 292.
[78] Act of 1836, 5 *Stat.* 117.   [79] *Ibid.*, sec. 6.

made to him" to purchase.[80] To indicate even more clearly that discrimination was intended, it was held in the case of *Tatham v. Lowber* that this clause did not apply to an American citizen when the latter was an assignee of an alien inventor and obtained letters patent in his own name for the assignment.

The fees charged for letters patent under this act were also discriminatory. If the applicant "be a citizen of the United States, or an alien who shall have been resident in the United States for one year next preceding, and shall have made oath of his intention to become a citizen thereof the sum of thirty dollars [was charged]; if a subject of the King of Great Britain, the sum of five hundred dollars; and all other persons the sum of three hundred dollars. . . ."[81]

The privilege of filing a caveat was also placed upon a discriminatory basis. This additional protection to one's invention was open only to a citizen of the United States and an alien "who shall have been resident in the United States one year next preceding, and shall have made oath of his intention to become a citizen thereof."[82]

In view of the fact that the above discriminations are to be found in the act, it is to be expected that the act should also require the applicant to make an oath as to his nationality. That the oath was an important part of the whole procedure was shown in the case of *Child v. Adams*. An alien who had received a patent had stated that he was a citizen of the United States when in fact he was an alien. It seems that any intention of fraud on the alien's part was absent. Judge Grier pointed out the fact that the fees paid by citizens and aliens who were residents for a year and had declared their intention to become citizens were quite different from those paid by other aliens. Under the provisions of the act the alien in this case was liable to a fee

[80] *Tatham v. Lowber* (1847), Fed. Cas. 13,764.
[81] Act of 1836, sec. 9.   [82] *Ibid.*, sec. 12.

of three hundred dollars instead of the thirty dollars that he paid. For this reason the court held that his patent was invalid "because the applicant did not comply with the conditions of the patent act in stating truly of what country he is a citizen."[83]

Some years later another case of misstatement of nationality arose. This case came under the Act of 1870,[84] which is to be discussed more fully below. However, it is not out of place to refer briefly to one of its provisions at this point; i.e., an applicant must state of what country he is a citizen.[85] An alien's patent was attacked upon the ground that he had made an incorrect statement as to his citizenship. Such an attack was held to be unavailing. The court was of the opinion that the act abolished "all such discriminations against aliens, and placed the latter upon the same footing as citizens, in respect to the grant of letters patent for inventions, and the enjoyment of the privileges thereby secured." The patent was held to be valid because "the citizenship of the applicant for a patent is no longer a matter of any real importance, and a mistake touching the same is harmless."[86]

Judge Acheson, who wrote the opinion just considered, was not correct in saying that "all such discriminations" against aliens had been abolished by the Act of 1870. The requirement that an alien patentee had to offer for sale his patented invention within a prescribed time had been abolished. Likewise, the Act of 1861 had abolished discriminations in fees charged for letters patent.[87] But the Act of 1870 did contain a discrimination as to those persons entitled to file a caveat. It retained the discrimination to be found in section 12 of the Act of 1836.[88]

---

[83] (1854), Fed. Cas. 2,673.
[84] 17 *Stat.* 198.   [85] *Ibid.,* sec. 30.
[86] *Tonduer v. Chambers* (1889), 37 Fed. 333.
[87] 12 *Stat.* 246, sec. 10.   [88] See above, p. 70.

To return to the Act of 1836, section 8 provided that an inventor was not entitled to a patent in the United States if the invention had been patented in a foreign country more than six months next preceding the filing of application in the United States. This restriction was removed by the Act of 1839, which provided:

That no person shall be debarred from receiving a patent for any invention or discovery, as provided in the act [of 1836] by reason of the same having been patented in a foreign country more than six months prior to his application: *Provided,* That the same shall not have been introduced into public and common use in the United States, prior to the application for such patent: *And provided also,* That in all cases every such patent shall be limited to the term of fourteen years from the date of publication of such foreign letter patent.[89]

The phrase "public and common use in the United States" referred to in the above quotation was required to extend to two years before the application.[90]

The "fourteen year" period of section 6 of the Act of 1839 was extended in a similar provision to seventeen years in the Act of 1861.[91] These provisions did not make an invention patentable in the United States because it had been patented abroad, "nor in any way found the patent here upon the patent there. The inventor could obtain a patent here by proving that he was the original and first inventor in this country, and complying with the laws of this country in making his application for it, and foreign use would have no effect upon it at all, and a prior foreign patent would have no effect *but to limit the term from its date.*"[92] Under these provisions American patents for inventions previously patented abroad were limited to seventeen years *from the date of publication of the foreign patent.*[93]

---

[89] 5 *Stat.* 353, sec. 6.
[90] *Ibid.,* sec. 7.   [91] 12 *Stat.* 246, sec. 16.
[92] *Cornely v. Marckwald* (1883), 17 Fed. 83. Italics mine.
[93] *De Florez v. Reynolds* (1880), 8 Fed. 434.

By 1870 the only discrimination that existed between citizen and alien was in the matter of filing a caveat. Even this discrimination no longer exists. The present *United States Code* grants the right to obtain a patent to "any person who has invented or discovered" any patentable invention and contains no limitation with respect to the citizenship of the inventor.[94] Hence, there is no limitation on the right of an inventor to obtain a patent by reason of his being a nonresident of the United States. Moreover, there is a still more liberal provision in that it is expressly provided by statute that "the executor or administrator *duly authorized by the laws of any foreign country* to administer upon the estate of a deceased inventor shall, in case such inventor was not domiciled in the United States at the time of his death, have the right to apply for and obtain the patent."[95]

3. *Trade-Marks:*—As in the case of copyrights and patents, there is a property right in connection with the possession and enjoyment of trade-marks.[96] Moreover, this property right is not based upon statutory but upon common law. Under the common law when a person adopted a mark to distinguish his productions from others offered in competition to his, and this distinguishing mark was used for a period of time and with a frequency sufficient to enable the consuming public to become acquainted with it and to learn to depend upon it as a guide in their purchase of material so marked, the merchant or producer who had adopted the mark acquired a property right in it. As other types of property rights, it was entitled to protection. Courts in this country can and have given protection to common law trade-marks.

There was no federal statute for the registration and protection of trade-marks until the Patent Act of 1870.[97] This legislation was declared unconstitutional by the United

---

[94] Tit. 35, sec. 31.   [95] *Ibid.*, sec. 46. Italics mine.
[96] *A. Bourjois & Co. v. Katzel* (1920), 274 Fed. 856.
[97] 17 *Stat.* 198, secs. 77 ff.

States Supreme Court because it was not limited to trade-marks used in commerce with foreign nations, or among the several states, or with the Indian tribes.[98] However, the courts have always given protection to common law trade-marks of citizens and aliens alike. Almost half a century before the first valid federal statute for the protection of trade-marks was enacted, a case arose in which a British firm sued, in the federal courts, an American firm for imitating their trade-mark. The American firm alleged that the British company had no right to sue because of its alienage. To this contention, Judge Story replied:

> First it is suggested, that the plaintiffs are aliens. Be it so. But in the courts of the United States, under the constitution and laws, they are entitled, being alien friends, to the same protection of their rights as citizens. . . . There is no difference between the case of a citizen and that of an alien friend, where his rights are openly violated.[99]

Here is an instance as early as 1844 of a federal court's offering protection to an alien's right to a common law trade-mark not on the basis of national treatment, but upon the broader basis of property, and holding that "in the courts of the United States, under the constitution and laws" aliens are entitled "to the same protection of their rights [property rights] as citizens."

Nor is this recognition (of an alien's right to establish and protect a common law trade-mark as being commensurate to the right of a citizen to do the same) peculiar to the federal courts. State courts likewise have recognized this right of aliens and have enforced the protection as against citizens, using as a basis the equality of alien and citizen to resort to the courts for the protection of their property.[100]

As a further indication of the fact that American appli-

---

[98] *Trade-Mark Cases* (1879), 100 U. S. 82.
[99] *Taylor v. Carpenter* (1844), Fed. Cas. 13,784. See also *Coffeen v. Brunton* (1849), Fed. Cas. 2,946.
[100] *Coats v. Holbrook* (1845), 2 Sand. Ch. (N. Y.) 586.

cation of the common law of trade-marks contemplates the equality of domiciled alien and citizen as resting exclusively upon municipal rather than international considerations, attention is directed to a case decided in 1846. An American suitor pleaded that an alien should not receive the protection of American courts unless the government of which the alien was a national extended protection to Americans. In this case *(Taylor v. Carpenter)* the court answered the contention as follows:

> But this might be good reason for legislation by Congress, not allowing aliens to have any rights, or to prosecute them in this court, unless they are reciprocal and allowed to our people in their respective countries. But no such discrimination has ever been made by Congress, and no court could make it by mere construction, without an exercise of judicial legislation. The cannibal of the Fejees [*sic*] may sue here in a personal action though having no courts at home for us to resort to. . . .
>
> An alien gets the right of protection from his obedience, industry, and care *while here,* and the usefulness of his capital and skill employed here, *when he resides abroad.*[101]

The first United States statute for the registration and protection of trade-marks which was sustained by the courts, was the Act of 1881.[102] These privileges were extended to citizens and resident aliens alike, and to nonresident aliens who were citizens or subjects of countries which extended national treatment to Americans in the matter of trademarks. Section 1 provides:

> That owners of trademarks used in commerce with foreign nations, or with the Indian tribes, provided such owners shall be domiciled in the United States, or located in any foreign country or tribes which by treaty, convention, or law, affords similar privileges to citizens of the United States, may obtain registration of such trademarks by complying with the following requirements. . . .

---

[101] (1846), Fed. Cas. 13,785. Italics mine.
[102] 21 *Stat.* 502.

The Act of 1881, however, contains a provision which prevents a foreigner's obtaining better than national treatment:

> That a certificate of registry shall remain in force for thirty years from its date; except in cases where the trademark is claimed for and applied to articles not manufactured in this country, and in which it receives protection under the laws of a foreign country for a shorter period, in which case it shall cease to have any force in this country by virtue of this act at the time that such trademark ceases to be exclusive property elsewhere.[103]

The act was supplemented the following year in order to give recognition to common law trade-marks, and to prevent any injustice toward those possessing such marks. It was provided "that nothing contained in the law [Act of 1881] shall prevent the registry of any lawful trademarks rightfully used by the applicant in foreign commerce or commerce with Indian tribes at the time of the passage of said act."[104]

The Acts of 1881 and 1882 extended national treatment to aliens domiciled in the United States, and to nonresident aliens if the government of the latter extended similar treatment to American citizens. It is to be noticed that the provision stated that owners of trade-marks *used* in commerce with foreign nations or with the Indian tribes may obtain registration of such trade-marks. In speaking of the acts, Judge Wallace said that they fortify the common law right to trade-marks by conferring statutory title upon the owner. The fact that the complainant is an alien does not affect his right of property in the mark. Property in trade-marks was not derived from the acts of Congress.[105]

In 1905 Congress repealed all former legislation relative to the registration and protection of trade-marks and enacted a more extensive statute upon the subject.[106] This act

---

[103] *Ibid.*, sec. 5.　　　　　　　[104] *22 Stat.* 298.
[105] *La Croix v. May* (1883), 15 Fed. 236.
[106] *35 Stat.* 724.

and several subsequent amendatory acts constitute a code of trade-mark law in this country. As was the case with the Act of 1881, the privilege of registration was accorded citizens and resident aliens upon absolute and unconditional equality. In the case of nonresident aliens, this privilege was extended upon the basis of reciprocity.[107]

The phrase "owner . . . located in any foreign country which by treaty, convention, or law, affords similar privileges to the citizens of the United States" has been interpreted by the courts. In the case of *J. & P. Baltz Brewing Co. v. Kaiserbrauerei, Beck & Co.,* the plaintiff, a German national, was seeking an injunction to restrain the defendant from using the word "Kaiser" in a trade-mark which had been used by the plaintiff. The defendant pointed out to the court that the laws of Germany and Austria did not permit the exclusive use of words as trade-marks. In other words, according to German and Austrian law, such a word as "Kaiser" to designate beer was open to common use. After citing that fact, the defendant called into evidence the fact that the United States had an international agreement with these two countries in which it was provided that recognition and protection of trade-marks would be extended by each of the contracting parties to the nationals of the other party upon a basis of equality with its own nationals. Then the defendant prayed the court to interpret this to mean that since Americans could not have exclusive use of such a word in Germany, then Germans would not be entitled to exclusive use in the United States. To this contention, the court replied that "the treaty stipulation only requires that the alien German should receive the same treatment as the American citizen" in the United States.[108] Hence the nonresident alien was entitled to protection of his mark upon the same basis as American citizens because his country extended national treatment to Americans in Germany.

[107] *Ibid.*, sec. 1.   [108] (1896), 74 Fed. 222.

There is another case in which the contention made by the defendant in the *Baltz* case was repeated. In *De Nobili v. Scanda*,[109] the plaintiff, a citizen and resident of Italy, brought suit against an American citizen for the infringement of trade-mark. There was a trade-mark understanding with Italy extending national treatment. The case was thrown out because both marks displayed flags of Italy and it is a violation of the laws of the United States to have national flags upon trade-marks. However, a dictum found in this case is pertinent here.

The court said: "Indeed, in all the acts of Congress on the subject, since the act of 1881, it seems that residents of foreign countries should have the right of protection of their trade-marks in the United States only when citizens of the United States could have protection for their trade-marks in the countries in which they were respectively citizens and residents." All of which is quite true. No one could deny that under American law nonresident aliens can receive protection of their marks only if protection is granted to Americans by the countries to which the aliens belong. However, the question naturally arises as to the nature of this protection. Does it mean that Italians are to be treated as Americans in the United States if Americans are treated as Italians in Italy? Or does it mean that Italians are to receive in the United States only protection exactly equal or commensurate with the protection extended by the Italian government to Americans in Italy? As was shown in the *Baltz* case, the court said that it meant the former. But in *De Nobili v. Scanda* the court said, in a dictum of course, that the latter was the correct interpretation. It was pointed out that in Italy the manufacture of tobacco was a government monopoly; hence a private individual, Italian or American, could not manufacture tobacco in Italy and, therefore, would have no need for or right to a trade-mark in this type of manu-

---

[109] (1912), 198 Fed. 341.

facture. Since the American's trade-mark for tobacco fabrication would amount to nothing in Italy, Italians had no right to receive protection in the United States for any mark used by them in the manufacture of tobacco.

It is suggested that Judge Orr, in the *De Nobili* case was confusing national treatment with extraterritorial effect of national legislation. The opinion of the court in the *Baltz* case is believed to be the correct and sound interpretation.

As was true in the Act of 1881, the Act of 1905 recognized the validity of common law trade-marks by providing:

> That nothing herein shall prevent the registration of any mark used by the applicant or his predecessors, or by those from whom title to the mark is derived, in commerce with foreign nations, or among the several states, or with the Indian tribes, which was in actual and exclusive use as a trade-mark of the applicant, or his predecessors from whom he derived title for ten years next preceding the passage of this act.[110]

Five years after this act was passed, a French company registered a trade-mark which it had been using in commerce between France and the United States since 1872. The registration was made in the United States Patent Office on November 1, 1910. A similar mark had already been registered by Rossmann and hence an interference developed. When the case reached the court, Garnier, the Frenchman, pointed out that although his registry had been subsequent to that of Rossmann, he (Garnier) had been making use of the mark in the United States long before ten years prior to the act of Congress. The court, depending upon section 5 of the Act of 1905, gave a verdict in favor of the alien and thereby recognized the alien's common law trade-mark although such recognition was detrimental to a citizen of the United States.[111]

Referring to this particular section of the act, the court

---

[110] 35 *Stat.* 724, sec. 5.
[111] *Rossmann v. Garnier* (1914), 211 Fed. 401.

in the case of *Scandinavia Belting Co. v. Asbestos & Rubber Works of America*[112] said: "That act does not prescribe what may be valid trade-marks, but simply permits the registration of trade-marks, and such registration in no way validates a trade-mark which was not previously valid." Is this not further recognition of the fact that validity of trade-marks is to be determined by the common law test of usage?

Section 27 of the Act of 1905 provides:

That no article of imported merchandise which shall copy or simulate the name of any domestic manufacture, or manufacturer, or trader, or of any manufacturer or trader located in any foreign country which, by treaty, convention, or law affords similar privileges to citizens of the United States, or which shall copy or simulate a trade-mark registered in accordance with the provisions of this act, or shall bear a name or mark calculated to induce the public to believe that the article is manufactured in the United States, or that it is manufactured in any foreign country or locality other than the country or locality in which it is in fact manufactured, shall be admitted to entry at any custom-house of the United States. . . .

This section was interpreted in the case of *Fred Gretsch Manufacturing Co. v. Schoening*.[113] The defendant was the American agent of a German manufacturer of violin strings by the name of Mueller. With Mueller's consent, Schoening registered the trade-mark used by Mueller, thereby making, so far as the United States government was concerned, the citizen Schoening the owner of the mark. The plaintiff bought violin strings from Mueller direct and had them shipped to the United States. Schoening, acting under section 27, had the customs authorities stop the shipment at the point of entry. The plaintiff was suing for release of his merchandise from the custody of the customs officials. The court decided in favor of the plaintiff because the court believed that "the obvious purpose of [section 27] is to

[112] (1919), 257 Fed. 937.   [113] (1916), 238 Fed. 780.

protect the public and to prevent any one from importing goods identified by their registered trade-mark which are not genuine."

It is suggested that such an interpretation could not be made today. The Act of 1930 provides:

It shall be unlawful to import into the United States any merchandise of foreign manufacture if such merchandise, or the label, sign, print, package, wrapper, or receptacle, bears a trademark owned by a citizen of, or by a corporation or association created or organized within the United States, and registered in the Patent Office by a person domiciled in the United States under the provisions of the Act [of 1905], as amended, if a copy of the certificate of registration of such trade-mark is filed with the Secretary of the Treasury, in the manner provided in Section 27 of such Act, unless written consent of the owner of such trade-mark is produced at the time of making entry.[114]

In 1906 Congress still further liberalized the Act of 1905 by making it possible for aliens whose countries did not extend reciprocity of protection to Americans to obtain protection for their marks in the United States. It was enacted:

That any owner of a trade-mark who shall have a manufacturing establishment within the territory of the United States, shall be accorded, so far as the registration and protection of trade-marks used on the products of such establishment are concerned, the same rights and privileges that are accorded to owners of trade-marks domiciled within the territory of the United States by the Act [of 1905].[115]

It is well recognized in the United States that trade-mark rights are not dependent on statutory enactment, but arise under common law from prior, exclusive appropriation and use. A trade-mark is a property right and any damage resulting from an infringement of this right may be prosecuted in the courts by *anyone* suffering such damage. The only discrimination in this country is against those nonresi-

---

[114] 46 *Stat.* 590, sec. 526.   [115] 34 *Stat.* 168, sec. 3.

dent aliens whose governments do not within their jurisdictions extend to American citizens national treatment in
the acquisition and protection of trade-marks. And even
these aliens if they have establishments in the United States,
although not themselves domiciled therein, are protected in
as full and ample a manner as citizens.

PROTECTION AGAINST ILLEGAL SEARCHES AND SEIZURES

A review of the cases forces one to the conclusion that
the constitutional protection against illegal searches and
seizures, found in the Federal Bill of Rights, extends in as
full and ample manner to aliens as it does to citizens. To
be sure, this extends protection in the matter of federal
activity only.[116] It is in no way binding upon the actions
of state officers in the performance of their duty. For protection against unreasonable searches and seizures by state
officials one must look to the several state constitutions. An
examination of these instruments proves that every state in
the union has provided for this protection in its fundamental
law. The great majority of them (forty-five) stipulate that
the "people" have the right to such protection, while the
remaining three employ the terms "subjects" and "citizens."[117]

The provision for this protection found in the United
States Constitution applies to citizens and aliens alike. A
federal court has expressed the opinion that "one of the most
fundamental of the 'body of liberties' guaranteed the *inhabitants* of the United States by our Constitution is freedom
from unreasonable search and seizure, and from arrest without due process." The court went on to say that "aliens
have constitutional rights. The Fourth, Fifth, Sixth and
Fourteenth Amendments are not limited in their applica-

---

[116] *Smith v. Maryland* (1855), 18 How. 71.

[117] Mass., I, 14 (subjects); N. H., Bill of Rights, 19 (subjects); West Va.,
III, 6 (citizens). As to application of Fourteenth Amendment see p. 84, below.

tion to citizens. They apply generally to all persons within the jurisdiction of the United States."[118]

In another federal case, the court was even more emphatic in the opinion that an alien, as well as a citizen, is entitled to this protection.

For the inalienable rights of personal security and safety, orderly and due process of law, are the fundamentals of the social compact, the basis of organized society, the essence and justification of government, the foundation key, and capstones of the Constitution. They are limited to no man, race, or nation, to no time, place or occasion, but belong to man always, everywhere, and in all circumstances.[119]

Most of the questions as to the applicability of the Fourth Amendment to aliens arise out of exclusion and deportation actions. The courts have held that exclusion proceedings, not being criminal in nature, are not subject to the restriction concerning searches and seizures. Therefore, in obtaining evidence to be used in such actions, federal officers are not obligated to consider the possible illegality of their searches.[120]

But once an alien is within the jurisdiction of the United States he comes within the protection of the Fourth Amendment. Any action brought by the government to procure his deportation cannot obtain conviction based upon evidence gotten in any manner which would be considered an illegal search and seizure. In such actions the alien enjoys the same protection as to the manner in which incriminating evidence may be obtained as is enjoyed by a citizen in any action to which the citizen may be party. Mr. Justice Brandeis, in a dictum, said: "It may be assumed that evidence obtained by the Department through an illegal search

[118] *Colyer v. Skeffington* (1920), 265 Fed. 17. Italics mine.
[119] *Ex parte Jackson* (1920), 263 Fed. 110.
[120] See *In re Chin Wah* (1910), 182 Fed. 256.

and seizure cannot be made the basis of a finding in deportation proceedings."[121]

In another deportation case the court held: "That the government can, by executive or judicial officers, exclude or expel aliens, is not in any manner to be questioned"; but aliens, while here, are entitled to the benefit of the guaranties of the Fourth and Fifth Amendments which "are not confined to citizens, as affecting liberties and property."[122]

There seems to be no doubt so far as the federal government is concerned that aliens receive protection equal to that accorded citizens in the matter of searches and seizures. No cases have been found in state courts expressing an opinion concerning the extent to which aliens are protected against state officials. In the state constitutional provisions relative to illegal searches and seizures, the majority extend this protection to the "people." As stated above, only three state constitutions employ the more restricted term of "citizen" or "subject."

Obviously that raises the question as to whether or not aliens receive different treatment in this matter in those states. Because of the lack of judicial decisions on the point it is necessary to resort to another method of answering the question.

There is no longer any dispute as to the applicability of the Fourteenth Amendment to the United States Constitution to aliens.[123] That is to say, the "due process of law" and the "equal protection of laws" clauses govern cases involving aliens as well as citizens. The amendment is a limitation upon the states. It is suggested that the three states, whose constitutional provisions for illegal searches and seizures are so phrased as to seem to extend this pro-

---

[121] *Bilokumsky v. Tod* (1923), 263 U. S. 149. See J. P. Clark, *Deportation of Aliens from the United States to Europe*, pp. 323-331.

[122] *U. S. v. Wong Quong Wong* (1899), 94 Fed. 832.

[123] *Colyer v. Skeffington*.

tection only to "citizens" or "subjects," could not discriminate in this matter against aliens because of the Fourteenth Amendment. In view of the many United States Supreme Court decisions on "due process" and "equal protection" of the laws, it is difficult to accept any other conclusion than that any discrimination in this matter on the part of the states would constitute a violation of the amendment. Therefore, aliens and citizens seem to be entitled to an equal protection against illegal searches and seizures by officers of both the federal and state governments.

IV

TREATMENT OF ALIENS IN THE
MATTER OF TAXATION

FEDERAL TAXATION

THE UNITED STATES laws of taxation make a distinction between citizens and aliens. Discrimination against aliens is
to be found in connection with income, estate, and gift
taxes. An examination of the nature of this discrimination
will be attempted in this section.

1. *Income tax:*—The earlier federal income tax statutes
did not apply to nonresident aliens. Only "residents of the
United States and citizens residing abroad" were liable to
taxation. In *Railroad Company v. Jackson,* Mr. Justice Nel-
son, referring to the phrase, said that nonresident aliens
"were not only not included in the description of persons
upon whom the tax was imposed, but were impliedly excluded by confining it to residents of the United States and
citizens residing abroad."[1]

All federal income tax statutes since the law of 1866
have placed a tax upon incomes of nonresident aliens.

The discrimination against aliens made by the various
federal income tax statutes applies only to a certain class of
aliens—nonresident aliens. The "status of resident aliens,
for income tax purposes, is the same as that of any other
individual."[2]

The law gives a citizen the advantage of more deductions from gross income than are allowed to nonresident

---

[1] (1868), 7 Wall. 262.
[2] *Van den Bosch v. Comm'r. of Internal Rev.* (1932), 26 United States Board
of Tax Appeals, Reports (hereinafter cited B.T.A.) 679.

aliens. But this is not necessarily a discrimination, and in some instances may in practice impose an even lighter tax burden than that imposed upon citizens or resident aliens because "in the case of a non-resident alien individual, gross income includes only the gross income from sources within the United States."[3]

In determining whether or not an alien is a resident, it has been held that the establishment of a domicile is not necessary to the acquisition of residence. The case of *Bowring v. Bowers*[4] involved a British subject who had not established a legal domicile in this country but who spent approximately twenty-two and a half years of a twenty-seven year period in the United States. The evidence convinced the court that there could be "no doubt that, in spite of his long stay in this country, his connections—family, social and business—were at all times peculiarly British." But despite this fact, the court went on to point out that "the United States Income Tax Acts, from the Act of 1913 on, have been uniform in levying a tax on the entire income of aliens, if resident here, and residence has been construed by the Commissioner in all his rulings as something which may be less than a domicile." The court upheld a long line of Treasury decisions to the effect that if an alien lives in the United States and has no *definite* intention as to his stay, or if he expects to return to his native country, but at some indefinite time in the future, he is to be considered a resident alien, which means that he may be taxed on his entire income.

An alien who has been nonresident and has an income derived from sources not within the United States, but who before the end of the tax year has become a resident of the United States, may not be taxed on such income. There is nothing in the law providing that if aliens become resident such income shall become subject to taxation.

[3] *U. S. C. A.,* Tit. 26, sec. 211(a). [4] (1928), 24 Fed. (2d) 918.

In the *Appeal of Ethel M. Codrington*,[5] the Commissioner of Internal Revenue forced the payment of the tax on the income received by a nonresident alien on shares of stock of the Canadian Pacific Railway Company. The Commissioner contended that the railroad company, having some miles of track and an office in the United States, was a resident foreign corporation, and hence any dividends paid by it to nonresident aliens were liable to the United States income tax law as income arising from a source within the United States. The Board of Tax Appeals could not accept this reasoning and said: "We think that it was never the intention of Congress to impose an income tax upon nonresident aliens in respect of income received from dividends of a foreign corporation practically all of whose property is located in a foreign country."

The statute phrase "from sources within the United States" has given rise to litigation. In the case of *De Ganay v. Lederer*[6] a nonresident alien protested the payment of tax on income from stocks and bonds issued by domestic corporations and from mortgages secured by domestic real estate. The Commissioner had collected the tax because the stock and bond certificates and mortgages were held by an agent in Pennsylvania. This agent had power of attorney and he was retained by the owner to sell and buy and manage in any way he saw fit. The alien claimed that stock certificates and mortgages were personal property and hence had situs only at the domicile of the owner and for that reason could not be taxed as income from sources within the United States. It was held that personal property of this type might be taxed where held. "It is difficult to conceive," said Mr. Justice Day speaking for the court, "how property could be more completely localized in the United States. There can be no question of the power of Congress to tax the income from such securities. Thus situated and held, and with the authority given to the local agent over them,

[5] (1927), 6 B. T. A. 415.   [6] (1919), 250 U. S. 376.

we think the income derived is clearly from property within the United States within the meaning of Congress as expressed in the statute under consideration."

The Board of Tax Appeals has upheld the Commissioner in taxing the dividends of a foreign corporation paid to nonresident aliens where the money which was the basis of these dividends was made in the United States. "The corporation's earnings within this country were the first cause or origin—the 'source'—of the subsequent dividends. It was the distribution of such earnings that Congress intended to tax for they were acquired within this country by the corporation under the protection which our laws afforded to its properties and operations."[7]

As showing further that the test of the taxability of income derived from dividends of corporate investment is origin of the income within the United States, another case concerning the taxation of dividends paid by a foreign corporation to a nonresident alien has arisen. In this case,[8] the bonds, upon the income on which the Commissioner claimed taxes, were held in the United States as security for a loan, but the money made by the corporation was made from business activity carried on outside the United States. The Board of Tax Appeals held:

It is immaterial that either temporarily or permanently the bond itself was within the jurisdiction of the United States. The income flowed from a source without the United States to a nonresident alien. It is of no consequence that it was routed through the City of Buffalo. The Fidelity Trust Co. of that city was merely a conduit through which the interest passed from one non-resident alien to another, and such interest is clearly not "gross income" within the meaning of the Revenue Act. . . .

Sale is necessary to the creation of an income. Manufacture has no influence upon determining the jurisdiction in

---

[7] *Lord Forres v. Comm'r. of Internal Rev.* (1932), 25 B. T. A. 154.
[8] *Appeal of L. E. McKinnon* (1927), 6 B. T. A. 412.

which the income originated. Goods of foreign manufacture which are sold in the United States constitute income from sources within the United States.[9]

In this connection a unique contention was made in the case of *Birkin v. Commissioner of Internal Revenue*.[10] The Commissioner taxed the plaintiff on the full amount of his sales in this country. Birkin protested this method of computing his tax. He claimed that the goods he sold in the United States had acquired a part of their sale price due to the fact that they were manufactured in England. The increment resulting from manufacture in England he proposed should be computed by determining the difference between the cost of manufacture abroad and the market value abroad of the articles at the time of exportation. The Board of Tax Appeals would not endorse this reasoning. "The profits are all brought about by sale here," and Birkin's income "includes the entire gain realized upon sale of goods in the ordinary course of business in this country, irrespective of where the increment has its situs." The fact of manufacture abroad does not reduce the profits obtained by sale within the United States.

A nonresident alien whose business comprises the purchase of goods in the United States to be sold abroad may not be taxed upon the income derived from such business even though he maintains an office in New York City. Such income is not from a source within the United States.[11] In support of this, the Board of Tax Appeals quoted with approval an opinion of the Attorney-General: "No income is derived from mere manufacture of goods; before there can be income there must be sale."[12]

The *Dorn* case, discussed in the paragraph immediately preceding, demonstrates very forcefully the liberality of the

[9] *Tootal Broadhurst Lee Co. v. Comm'r. of Internal Rev.* (1929), 30 Fed. (2d) 239.   [10] (1926), 5 B. T. A. 402.
[11] *Dorn v. Comm'r. of Internal Rev.* (1928), 12 B. T. A. 1102.
[12] 32 *Op'ns. Att'y. Gen'l.* 336.

policy of the United States government in taxing aliens. On September 9, 1921, Dorn had admitted the manager of his New York office to partnership. It was held that the manager, a resident of the United States (the opinion fails to state whether he was a citizen or resident alien, but that is of no consequence because these two classes are treated alike), was liable to income tax in respect to his pro rata share of the profits of the partnership, but that the nonresident alien partner was exempt from income tax in respect to his share of the profits.[13]

It has been stated above, and discussed at some length, that manufacture plays no part in determining the source of the income derived from sale of goods. It has also been shown that the profits from goods manufactured in this country and sold abroad are not taxable income in this country. However, it has been held that royalties received by a nonresident alien singer from the *foreign* sales of phonograph records made in the United States were taxable as income derived from a source within this country.[14]

Interest paid on an open account by a resident individual to a nonresident alien is income from sources in the United States.[15]

Profit made on the sale of Liberty Bonds has also been held to be taxable income. Some of these bonds were purchased on the open market below par for a nonresident individual who was not engaged in business in the United States. The bonds were redeemed at par, thereby giving the alien holder a profit. The Commissioner taxed this profit as income from a source within the United States. It was contended that the Commissioner of Internal Revenue was in error in levying a tax on this profit because section 4 of the Act of March 3, 1919, exempts the principal and interest of

[13] *Dorn v. Comm'r. of Internal Rev.*
[14] *Ingram v. Bowers* (1932), 57 Fed. (2d) 65.
[15] *Motty Eitingon v. Comm'r. of Internal Rev.* (1933), 27 B. T. A. 1341.

the Second Liberty Bonds from taxation.[16] The Board of Tax Appeals held that the tax was not levied upon the principal obtained by redemption, but upon the profit resulting from the purchase of the bonds below par and redeeming them at par.[17]

It was stated earlier in the chapter that resident aliens receive treatment equal to that accorded citizens in the matter of income taxation. This is not entirely correct. There is one slight difference of treatment in connection with the right of the person to deduct taxes paid to other governments. The status of the individual determines the extent to which he may deduct these taxes from his gross income. A citizen of the United States regardless of residence may take as a credit "any income, war-profits, and excess-profits taxes paid or accrued during the taxable year to any foreign country or to any possession of the United States." An alien, resident in the United States, may also deduct taxes paid or due the government of any possession of the United States. However, he may deduct taxes paid to foreign countries *only* "if the foreign country of which such alien resident is citizen or subject, in imposing such taxes, allows a similar credit to citizens of the United States residing in such country."[18] In other words, a condition of reciprocity must exist before he is allowed to reduce his gross income by means of a credit for taxes paid the foreign country. Other than this minor discrimination, a resident alien is placed upon an equal footing with a citizen.

Much greater discrimination is made in the income tax provisions relating to nonresident aliens. In this connection the law provides two kinds of treatment. If the nonresident alien is engaged in trade or business in the United States he receives more favorable treatment than does a nonresident alien not so engaged in business. The former is taxed upon

[16] 40 *Stat.* 1311.
[17] *Hubert De Stuers v. Comm'r. of Internal Rev.* (1932), 26 B. T. A. 201.
[18] *U. S. C. A.,* Tit. 26, sec. 131.

his net income at the same rate as a citizen or resident of this country. However, he does not receive national treatment in that he is placed in a less favorable position in determining his net income. It is true that this type of nonresident alien's gross income is only that income derived from sources within the United States, whereas a citizen or resident's gross income is comprised of income from whatever sources derived. This gives an advantage to the nonresident alien. This advantage, however, is offset by the fact that he is not allowed as many deductions in determining the net taxable income. He is entitled to a personal exemption of only $1,000 and receives no credit for dependents unless he is a resident of a contiguous country.[19] In the second place, he is not allowed any credit for taxes paid to foreign governments or to the governments of the possessions of the United States.[20]

There is some discrimination against nonresident aliens engaged in business in the United States in the matter of deductions as well as in connection with the credits discussed above. All deductions allowed to citizens and resident aliens are allowed to such nonresident aliens, but only to the extent to which they are connected in some way with income from the United States. In clarification of this last statement, a rather long quotation is believed justifiable:

(a) In the case of a non-resident alien individual the deductions shall be allowed only if and to the extent that they are connected with income from sources within the United States; and the proper apportionment and allocation of the deductions with respect to sources of income within and without the United States shall be determined as provided in section 119, under rules and regulations prescribed by the Commissioner with the approval of the Secretary.

(b) Losses.

(1) The deduction for losses not connected with the trade or business if incurred in transactions entered into for profit, al-

<hr/>

[19] *Ibid.*, sec. 213. [20] *Ibid.*, sec. 215.

lowed by section 23 (e) (2) shall be allowed whether or not connected with income from sources within the United States, but only if the profit, if such transaction had resulted in a profit, would be taxable under this chapter.

(2) The deduction for losses of property not connected with the trade or business if arising from certain casualties or theft, allowed by section 23 (e) (3), shall be allowed whether or not connected with income from sources within the United States, but only if the loss is of property within the United States.

(c) The so-called "charitable contributions" deduction allowed by section 23 (o) shall be allowed whether or not connected with income from sources within the United States, but only as to contributions or gifts made to domestic corporations, or to community chests, funds, or foundations, created in the United States, or to the vocational rehabilitation fund.[21]

The income tax laws treat those nonresident aliens engaged in business in the United States more liberally than is the case with nonresident aliens not so engaged in business. In addition to more liberal treatment in the matters of credits and deductions, the law exempts income of a nonresident alien which is derived from international shipping. The income of a nonresident alien which "consists exclusively of earnings from the operation of a ship or ships documented under the laws of a foreign country which grants an equivalent exemption to citizens of the United States and to corporations organized in the United States, shall not be included in the gross income and shall be exempt from taxation."[22]

[21] Ibid., sec. 212.

[22] Ibid., sec. 211(b). Executive agreements for relief from double income tax on shipping profits have been entered into with the following governments: Japan, Mar. 31, 1926 and June 8, 1926, 47 Stat. 2578; Canada, Aug. 2, 1928 and Sept. 17, 1928, ibid., 2580; Spain, Apr. 16, 1930 and June 10, 1930, ibid., 2584; Great Britain and Northern Ireland, Aug. 11, 1924, Nov. 18, 1924, Nov. 24, 1924, Jan. 15, 1925, Feb. 13, 1925, Mar. 16, 1925, ibid., 2587; Netherlands, Sept. 13, 1926, Oct. 19, 1926, Nov. 27, 1926, ibid., 2601; France, June 11, 1927, July 8, 1927, ibid., 2604; Greece, Feb. 29, 1928, Apr. 26, 1928, Apr. 2, 1929, June 10, 1929, ibid., 2608; Denmark and Iceland, May 22, 1922, Aug. 9 and 18, 1922, Oct. 24, 25, 28, 1922, Dec. 5 and 6, 1922, ibid., 2612;

In order to prevent abuse of the phrase "engaged in trade or business within the United States," the law provides that although normally the phrase comprehends the performance of personal services within the United States, it is not to be interpreted to include the performance of personal services for a nonresident alien individual, foreign partnership, or foreign corporation, not engaged in trade or business within the United States, by a nonresident alien individual temporarily present in the United States for a period or periods not exceeding a total of ninety days during the taxable year and whose compensation for such services does not exceed in the aggregate $3,000.[23] The intention of this provision is "to permit residents of other countries to make brief visits to the United States for business purposes such as the buying and selling of goods, without being subject, before leaving the country, to a demand for a payment of tax on their compensation during the period of their stay here." Numerous cases of this sort arising under the old law "created an ill will quite disproportionate to the slight revenue involved."[24]

If the nonresident alien receiving income from sources within the United States is not engaged in business in this country he is subject to one of two treatments. The size of the income determines which of the two shall be applied.

A nonresident alien not engaged in business in the United States is not taxed upon profits derived from transactions on the stock and commodity markets or profits from the sale within the United States of any other real or personal property. The reason for exempting him from tax-

Norway, Nov. 26, 1924, Jan. 23, 1925, Mar. 24, 1925, *ibid.*, 2617; Brazil, Mar. 5, 1929, May 31, 1929, Sept. 17, 1929, Mar. 11, 1930, Aug. 21, 1930, Sept. 1, 1930, *ibid.*, 2620; Germany, Sept. 5, 1923, Oct. 8, 1923, Jan. 19, 1924, May 5, 1924, Sept. 3, 1924, Nov. 29, 1924, Dec. 11, 1924, Mar. 20, 1925, *ibid.*, 2627; Italy, Mar. 10, 1926, May 5, 1926, *ibid.*, 2599; Irish Free State, Aug. 24, 1933, Jan. 9, 1934, 48 *Stat.* 90. See, M. B. Carroll, "The Development of International Tax Law," 29 *Amer. Journ. Int'l. Law*, 586-597.

[23] *Internal Revenue Code, 1939*, sec. 119(a)(3).
[24] *Senate Reports*, No. 2156, p. 21, 74 Cong., 2 Sess.

ation on such capital gains is that it was "found administratively impossible effectively to collect this tax."[25] The tax is levied upon interest (except interest on deposits with persons carrying on the banking business), dividends, rents, salaries, wages, premiums, annuities, compensations, remunerations, emoluments, or other fixed or determinable annual or periodical gains, profits and income.[26] In other words, only the income from these specified sources is subject to taxation.

The size of the income received from the sources indicated above determines which of two possible treatments shall be applied. If the alien receives an income of less than $21,600, he is taxed at a flat rate of ten per centum upon his entire income.[27] He is not allowed any credits or deductions.[28] However, "such rate shall be reduced, in the case of a resident of a contiguous country, to such rate (not less than 5 per centum) as may be provided by treaty with such country."[29]

Prior to the Act of 1937 all nonresident aliens not engaged in business in the United States were taxed at the rate of ten per centum upon their gross incomes. Under such an arrangement persons with unusually high incomes actually paid less income taxes than before. "In fact," said the House Committee, "it has permitted certain former citizens of the United States now citizens of other countries, but who derive a large amount of income from sources within the United States either directly or through an American trust, to pay substantially less Federal income tax than they paid under prior revenue acts."[30] In other words, if these

[25] *Ibid.*

[26] *Internal Revenue Code, 1939*, sec. 211(a)(1)(A).

[27] *Ibid.*

[28] *Treas. Reg.*, No. 94, Art. 213-1, as amended by *Treas. Decision*, 4791, Jan. 14, 1938.

[29] The rate for Canadians is 5% as a result of a treaty with Canada, Aug. 13, 1937, *U. S. Treaty Series*, No. 920.

[30] *House Reports*, No. 1546, 75 Cong., 1 Sess.

individuals had been subject to both normal and surtaxes the effective rate of tax on their income from sources within the United States would have been much higher than the ten per centum under the Act of 1936. To remedy this situation, the Act of 1937 provided a different treatment for persons receiving an income of over $21,600. This figure was chosen because it is the approximate point at which the effective rate of taxation (normal and surtaxes) becomes ten per centum.

As the law stands, an alien receiving over $21,600 must compute his tax two ways and pay the higher of the two. In the first place he is to subtract from the gross income the credits to which he is entitled. These are a personal exemption of $1,000 and, if a resident of a contiguous country, $400 for each dependent. He is also entitled to the same deductions allowed an alien engaged in business in the United States.[31] After taking these credits and making these deductions from the gross income, the tax is computed at the same rates for normal and surtaxes that are applicable to a citizen or resident. If the amount of the tax resulting from such computation is more than ten per centum of the *gross* income, that is the amount to be paid. If, however, it is less, then the tax levied is ten per centum of the gross income.[32]

2. *Gift tax:*—Another federal tax in which discrimination against aliens is to be found is the gift tax. This is a variable tax placed upon gifts, which is graduated according to the value of the property given. As in the case of the income tax, the discrimination to be found in the gift tax is not a discrimination as between citizen and *resident* alien, but as between citizen and resident on the one hand and the nonresident alien on the other.

The first federal gift tax was enacted in 1924.[33] This

[31] See above, pp. 93 f.
[32] *Internal Revenue Code, 1939,* sec. 211(c).
[33] 43 *Stat.* 253.

legislation was repealed by the Revenue Act of 1926,[34] and there was no federal tax levied on gifts until the enactment of the Revenue Act of 1932.[35]

Due to the comparative recency of this type of taxation, there has not been time for the development of any extensive body of court decisions. Some litigation did result from the Act of 1924, but a case concerning the subject matter of this study, alien rights, has not been found. Therefore, discussion must be confined to a consideration of the legislation itself without the aid of court decisions as guides to proper conclusions.

Attention has already been directed to the fact that federal legislation relative to taxation of gifts makes no discrimination as between citizens of the United States and aliens resident in the United States. "For the calendar year 1932 and each calendar year thereafter a tax, computed as provided in section 502, shall be imposed upon the transfer during such calendar year by any individual, resident or non-resident, of property by gift."[36] The tax is levied upon a transfer of property "by any individual, resident or non-resident." If the person is a citizen or a resident of the United States, any transfer by him of property located anywhere in the world is taxable, "but in the case of a non-resident not a citizen of the United States, [the tax] shall apply to a transfer *only if the property is within the United States*."[37]

A Treasury Department regulation provides that "a resident is one who has his domicile in the United States at the time of the gift. All others are non-residents. A person acquires a domicile in a place by living there for even a brief period of time with no definite present intention of moving therefrom."[38] This definition is important only in so far as it applies to aliens. A citizen, whether he is resident

[34] *44 Stat.* 9.
[35] *47 Stat.* 169.
[36] Act of 1932, sec. 501(a).
[37] *Ibid.*, sec. 501(b). Italics mine.
[38] *Treas. Reg.* No. 79, Art. 4.

or nonresident, is taxed upon whatever taxable gifts he makes, regardless of where the property has its situs. But if an alien is a resident of the United States he is entitled to all the deductions that a citizen enjoys in computing his tax. If the alien is not a resident of the United States he does not receive treatment equal to that of a citizen in the matter of deductions to which he is entitled.

When "property is situated within the United States," it has been provided:

Real estate and tangible personal property physically located in the United States constitute property having a situs in the United States. Intangible personal property, such as a bond, share of stock, note, insurance contract, simple debt, or other chose in action, has a situs in the United States if consisting of a property right issuing from or enforceable against a corporation (public or private) organized in the United States or a person who is a resident of the United States. Intangible personal property also has a situs in the United States if the certificate of stock, bond, bill, note, or other written evidence of such property, which is customarily treated as being the property itself, is physically located in the United States, whether such certificate of stock, bond, etc., was issued by a resident or non-resident of the United States.[39]

The discrimination against aliens found in the gift tax is in connection with the deductions that may be made. The tax is placed upon "net gifts" for a calendar year and this is arrived at by making the deductions provided in the statute. A nonresident alien is not permitted to make all the deductions allowed a resident person.

A citizen or resident alien is entitled to an exemption of $40,000.[40] This is not allowed a nonresident alien. The amount of the "net gifts" of a nonresident alien is computed by deduction from the value of the property situated in the United States which was the subject of the gift only the

[39] *Ibid.*, Art. 18.
[40] Act of 1935, 49 *Stat.* 1014, sec. 301(b).

value of the property which was given for public, charitable, and other uses to be discussed below. As will be seen, gifts for public, charitable, religious and other such uses are deductible for either the alien or the citizen, for the resident or the nonresident.

In addition to denying the nonresident alien the specific exemption of $40,000, there is a further discrimination in the other items of deduction, these items are upon the same general subject matter, regardless of whether the person is a citizen or a nonresident alien. In other words, there are several instances where both classes are allowed deductions of gifts made for the same purpose, but the nonresident alien is more restricted. A citizen or a resident alien, in addition to the specific exemption, may deduct gifts made to the "United States, any State or Territory, or any political subdivision thereof, or the District of Columbia, for exclusively public purposes."[41] Gifts made to corporations, trusts, or fraternal organizations for scientific, literary, or educational purposes are deductible.[42] One may deduct gifts to organizations of war veterans if no part of the net earnings of such organizations "inures to the benefit of any private shareholder or individual."[43]

The nonresident alien likewise may deduct gifts made to the organizations and agencies just mentioned. The right to deduct such items is governed by the same rules as those applying to gifts made by citizens and residents of the United States. However, this right is subject to two exceptions. Whereas the citizen and resident may deduct gifts made to *any* corporation engaged in charitable or religious work regardless of where such corporation is located, the nonresident may deduct only those gifts made to corporations incorporated in the United States or a state thereof.[44]

---

[41] Act of 1932, sec. 505(a)(2)(A).

[42] *Ibid.*, sec. 505(a)(2)(B), as amended by Act of 1934, 48 *Stat.* 680, sec. 517(a); and Act of 1932, sec. 505(a)(2)(C).

[43] *Ibid.*, sec. 505(a)(2)(D) & (E).

[44] *Ibid.*, sec. 505(b)(2), as amended by Act of 1934, sec. 517(a).

The second discrimination in this connection is that if the nonresident alien's gift is made, for example, to a community chest or lodge, it must be for use within the United States and for the purposes specified in the statutory provision.[45]

3. *Estate tax:*—The federal estate tax applies to citizens and aliens. There is no discrimination as between resident citizen and resident alien; both are taxed upon the same basis. However, discriminations are to be found in this tax. The basis of the tax is the Revenue Act of 1926.[46] This law as originally enacted discriminated between resident and nonresident, regardless of citizenship. This naturally may not be considered as a discrimination against aliens. Later legislation has amended the act so that a definite discrimination against aliens has been accomplished. The Revenue Act of May 10, 1934,[47] substituted for the phrase "non-resident decedent," the phrase "non-resident not a citizen of the United States" wherever it appeared in the Act of 1926. As is quite evident, this brought about a discrimination against aliens. But it is to be kept in mind that the discrimination applies only to one class of aliens, that is, to nonresident aliens. As was the case in the income tax and gift tax, this discrimination is not in the nature of a discriminatory burden because here also the taxable property is not based upon the whole estate, but only upon that part to be found in the United States at the time of the alien's death.

The tax is estimated upon the net estate left by the deceased. Discrimination against nonresident aliens is made in the determination of the net estate. A nonresident alien is not allowed as many deductions from his gross estate. As stated above, this discrimination in the matter of deductions allowable applied until very recently to nonresident citizens as well as nonresident aliens. So in the last analysis, there

[45] Act of 1932, sec. 505(b)(3), as amended by Act of 1934, sec. 517(b).
[46] 44 *Stat.* 9.
[47] 48 *Stat.* 680, sec. 403(b), (c), and (d).

was no discrimination between citizens and aliens similarly situated. Discrimination exists today only as between nonresident citizen and nonresident alien, and this has been in effect only since the going into effect of the Act of 1934. Obviously then, the whole problem of discrimination centers upon the matter of residence. The courts have held that residence in the United States, and hence the right to all deductions allowable under the law, is determined by the intention of the party concerned.

An Englishman inherited some land in Wyoming, came to this country, and built a home in Laramie. The court found that in all of his activity he considered Laramie as his home. He paid taxes there and took part in the local affairs. Three months after his arrival, however, he returned to England to practice for an automobile race in which he had been entered before he left England for Wyoming. While preparing for the race he was killed. The government classified him as a nonresident alien and hence entitled to fewer deductions than he would be entitled to as a resident. The court held that the Englishman's estate was entitled to all the deductions allowable under the law to a resident alien or citizen. He was held to be a resident for the purposes of the estate tax because "intention is the governing factor in determining domicile."[48]

The taxable estate of a nonresident alien is determined by making the deductions allowed to this class of persons from the value of that part of the gross estate *which at the time of death is situated in the United States.*[49] Such a reduction of a nonresident alien's estate renders whatever discrimination exists of much less importance.

An explanation of "that part of his gross estate which at the time of his death is situated in the United States" can be most clearly explained by quoting the article of the

[48] *Cooper v. Reynolds* (1927), 24 Fed. (2d) 150.
[49] *U. S. C. A.*, Tit. 26, sec. 1095(b).

Regulations pertaining to this matter. Article 50 is as follows:

Real estate and tangible personal property are situated in the United States if physically therein. Certificates of stock, bonds, bills, notes and other written evidences of intangible property which are treated as being the property itself are property situated in the United States if physically situated therein.

Except as provided in section 303 (e) intangible personal property has a situs within the United States if consisting of a property right issuing from or enforceable against a corporation (public or private) organized in the United States or a person who is a resident of the United States.[50]

There are also certain statutory exclusions in this connection. The amount receivable as insurance upon the life of a nonresident alien and any money deposited with any person carrying on the banking business, by or for a nonresident alien who was not engaged in business in the United States at the time of his death, is not deemed "property within the United States."[51]

It is to be noticed that so far as bank deposits are concerned two conditions must prevail. The money must be deposited with someone "carrying on the banking business." It has been held that a brokerage house which does not carry on a regular banking business, whose primary function is the marketing of stocks and bonds, but which does cash checks and perform certain other services of convenience, is not a company carrying on a banking business within the meaning of such a statutory provision.[52] The second condition is that the decedent must not have been engaged in business in the United States at the time of his death.[53]

[50] *Treas. Reg.* No. 80.
[51] Act of 1926, sec. 403(e), as amended by Act of 1934.
[52] *Todd v. U. S.* (1931), 46 Fed. (2d) 589.
[53] For decisions relative to this point see *Burnet v. Brooks* (1933), 288 U. S. 378; *Turner v. McCuen*, D. Ct. of Vt., Aug. 30, 1930. The second case is an unreported one which may be found in 9 *Amer. Fed'l. Tax Rep'ts.* 1664.

There has been some litigation arising out of the question of the situs of stocks and bonds. For purposes of the estate tax, the maxim *mobilia sequuntur personam* does not prevail. The United States Supreme Court has held it well established that the taxing power of Congress could reach securities held by a nonresident which were physically in the United States. Such stocks and bonds are included in the nonresident alien's gross estate which is located in the United States.[54]

As to the deductions that the various provisions allow, a resident, citizen or alien, is entitled to the specific exemption. This exemption is also allowed a citizen, regardless of residence, if the decedent died after 11:40 A.M. Eastern Standard Time, May 10, 1934 (the time prescribed for the entering into effect of the act). The nonresident alien is not allowed any specific exemption whatsoever.[55]

The first kinds of deductions which are allowed to the nonresident alien (or nonresident regardless of citizenship if the decedent died before the enactment of the Act of 1934) are expenses incurred by the funeral, administration of the estate, claims against the estate, and various losses resulting from fire, storm, shipwreck, or other such casualty.[56] The Act of 1926 specifically placed a limit upon the amount of deduction for such expenses and claims. The nonresident had to proportion these expenses and was entitled to deduct only that proportion of the expenses and claims which was equal to that proportion of his gross estate situated in the United States, "but in no case [was] the amount so deducted [to] exceed ten per centum of the value of that part of his gross estate which at the time of his death [was] situated in the United States."[57]

[54] *Burnet v. Brooks.* See also, *First Nat'l. Bank of Boston v. Comm'r. of Internal Rev.* (1933), 63 Fed. (2d) 685. For an earlier lower court decision holding the contrary see *Shenton v. U. S.* (1931), 53 Fed. (2d) 249.
[55] See *Treas. Reg.* No. 80, Art. 48.
[56] Act of 1926, sec. 303(a) (1).   [57] *Ibid.*, (b)(1).

The placing of a limitation of ten per centum as the maximum value for this particular deduction was attacked as unconstitutional. Judge Learned Hand, while believing it unfair to place such a limit, was of the opinion that it was constitutional.[58] Subsequent legislation removed this discriminatory limit upon the deductions of nonresidents by striking from the provision the clause just quoted.[59]

Nevertheless, in spite of the removal of the limitation, there still remain several differences of treatment as between resident and nonresident, or as between citizen and resident alien on the one hand and nonresident alien on the other, since the Act of 1934. While the maximum amount deductible is no longer limited to a specific amount, the nonresident (before the Act of 1934) or the nonresident alien (after that act) may deduct "only that proportion of the aggregate thereof . . . which the value of that part of the gross estate situated in the United States, bears to the value of the entire gross estate, wherever situated."[60] The second difference in treatment is that "no deduction shall be allowed in the case of a non-resident [alien since the Act of 1934] unless the executor includes in the return required to be filed . . . the value at the time of his death of that part of the gross estate of the non-resident [alien since the Act of 1934] not situated in the United States."[61]

The right to deduct the value of the property that a nonresident alien has received by gift, devise, bequest or inheritance is, in the main, governed by the same rules that apply to such deductions when made by a resident or citizen, except for several minor considerations. The property for which the deduction is claimed must be included in that part of the decedent's gross estate which is situated in the United States at the time of his death. A second difference

[58] *City Bank Farmer's Trust Co. v. Bowers* (1934), 68 Fed. (2d) 909.
[59] Act of 1928, 45 *Stat.* 791, sec. 401(a).
[60] *Treas. Reg.* No. 80, Art. 52.   [61] Act of 1926, sec. 303(c).

of treatment is that when a nonresident alien has received a gift or legacy from some prior decedent, the tax upon which has been "paid in whole or in part prior to the decedent's death, then the deduction allowable . . . shall be reduced by the amount so paid." Furthermore, the "deduction allowable under this paragraph shall be reduced by an amount which bears the same ratio to the amounts allowable as deductions under paragraph (1) [concerning funeral expenses and claims upon the estate] and (3) [concerning gifts to governments and charities] of this subdivision as the amount otherwise deductible under this paragraph bears to the value of that part of the decedent's gross estate which at the time of his death is situated in the United States."[62] And in the third place, this deduction is not available to any extent unless the executor includes in the return the value at the time of the decedent's death of that part of the gross estate not situated in the United States.[63]

The value of the property transferred for public and charitable purposes is a third deduction that is allowed to citizens, residents, and nonresident aliens. However, the nonresident alien does not receive as much latitude in making the deduction. His right is limited to the transfers of property to corporations or associations created or organized in the United States, or to trustees for use in the United States.[64] As is true of all deductions allowed to nonresident aliens, this particular one also is available only if the executor includes in the return the value at the time of the decedent's death of that part of the gross estate not situated in the United States.[65]

4. *Summarizing statement:*—There is no difference of treatment in federal taxation as to citizens and resident aliens. The only discriminations existing in the entire field

---

[62] Act of 1932, 47 *Stat.* 169, sec. 806(b), as amended by Act of 1934, sec. 402.   [63] Act of 1926, sec. 303(c).

[64] *Ibid.,* (b)(3), as amended by Act of 1932, sec. 807 and Act of 1934. sec. 406.   [65] Act of 1926, sec. 303(c).

of federal taxation are to be found in the income, gift, and estate taxes. The discrimination here is between the treatment accorded citizens and resident aliens on the one hand and nonresident aliens on the other. This can hardly be considered as a penalization of nonresident aliens when one bears in mind that when applying these three forms of taxation to citizens and resident aliens all of their property, wherever situated, is taken as the base for computation. Looking at the problem exclusively from the tax basis point of view, a nonresident alien receives better treatment because only a portion of his property is taken into consideration. It is only reasonable that some difference of treatment be accorded in order to counterbalance the advantage that the nonresident alien enjoys.

STATE TAXATION

In the exercise of its taxing power, the federal government does not discriminate against resident aliens. Some discrimination is found in state tax laws. An alien may be charged a higher fee for hunting and fishing licenses.[66] Likewise, states have discriminated in their inheritance tax laws. This latter discrimination has not been—and could not be—against resident aliens, but has been confined to nonresident aliens.

States are prohibited by the provisions of the Fourteenth Amendment to the United States Constitution from discriminating against resident aliens. "Persons" as used in the amendment has been construed to include aliens as well as citizens of the United States.[67] Moreover, a federal court has held:

The Fourteenth Amendment imposes a limitation by "equal protection" upon the exercise of all the powers of the state which can touch the individual or his property, including that of taxa-

[66] See below, pp. 133 ff.

[67] *Yick Wo v. Hopkins* (1886), 118 U. S. 356. See also *Fraser v. McConway* (1897), 82 Fed. 257; *State v. Montgomery* (1900), 47 Atl. (Me.) 165.

tion. . . . The equal protection of the laws to any one implies not only that the means for the security of his private rights shall be accessible to him on the same terms with others, but also that he shall be exempt from any greater burdens or charges than such as are equally imposed upon all others under like circumstances. This equal protection forbids unequal exactions of any kind, and among them that of unequal taxation.[68]

The discrimination that is found in state inheritance tax laws is a legal discrimination because it is applied to nonresident aliens. The protection of the Fourteenth Amendment is extended only to persons who are physically present within the territorial jurisdiction of the state.[69] The validity of a state statute which charges a higher tax for property going to alien heirs who do not reside in the United States has been upheld by the United States Supreme Court before the adoption of the Fourteenth Amendment. Such a law is "nothing more than an exercise of the power which every State and sovereignty possesses, of regulating the manner and terms upon which property real or personal within its dominion may be transmitted by last will and testament, or by inheritance; and of prescribing who shall and who shall not be capable of taking it." The court went on to say that, since the state unquestionably could determine who could receive property in this manner, the state could also place conditions under which persons could receive property. The tax was held valid.[70]

It would seem that the states are free to discriminate against nonresident alien heirs and that such discrimination would not fall under the limitation of the Fourteenth Amendment. However, is the federal government, through its treaty-making power, able to extend to nonresident alien

[68] *County of Santa Clara v. Southern Pacific R.R. Co.* (1883), 18 Fed. 385. See also *Railroad Tax Cases* (1882), 13 Fed. 722.

[69] *State v. Travelers' Insurance Co.* (1898), 40 Atl. (Conn.) 465.

[70] *Mager v. Grima* (1849), 8 How. 490.

heirs national treatment in the matter of inheritance taxes? That government has entered into a number of commercial and other treaties which devote a large number of their provisions to the matter of national treatment upon a reciprocal basis. Among the provisions is a rather common one to the effect that the citizens or subjects of one contracting party shall enjoy in the jurisdiction of the other the same privileges relative to inheritance as are enjoyed by the nationals of the second party. What effect does such a treaty provision have upon the inheritance tax discrimination that is found in some state laws?

The discrimination which existed in the Louisiana inheritance tax law was upheld in the case of *Mager v. Grima,* discussed above. But this case did not involve the interpretation of a treaty provision. At the time this case was decided the United States had entered into no treaty with France providing national treatment in the matter of inheritance.

Consideration of the effect of treaties upon state inheritance tax laws which discriminate against nonresident aliens must be approached from two points of view: when the decedent is a citizen of the United States, and when the decedent is a resident alien.

One of the earlier state inheritance tax statutes which gave rise to litigation was that of Louisiana. This statute placed a discriminatory tax on property left to a person resident without the United States. However, it was levied, and at the same rate, against property going to a nonresident citizen of Louisiana as well as against property going to a nonresident alien.[71]

A citizen and resident of Louisiana left some property to a citizen of Württemberg. The state taxed the property, and the heir opposed payment on the ground that it violated his treaty right. Article III of the treaty in question provided that:

[71] *State v. Poydras* (1854), 9 La. Ann. 165.

The citizens or subjects of each of the contracting parties shall
have power to dispose of their personal property within the States
of the other, by testament, donation, or otherwise, and their heirs,
legatees, and donees, being citizens or subjects of the other contracting party, shall succeed to their said personal property, and
may take possession thereof, either by themselves, or by others
acting for them, and dispose of the same at their pleasure, paying
such duties only as the inhabitants of the country where the said
property lies, shall be liable to pay in like cases.[72]

The case went to the United States Supreme Court, and
the court said: "we concur with the supreme court of
Louisiana in the opinion that the treaty does not regulate
the testamentary dispositions of citizens or subjects of the
contracting powers in reference to property within the country of their origin or citizenship." The court went on to
say that since the law applied equally to citizens of Louisiana
when resident abroad, the equality which is the basis of
national treatment has not been violated by the law in question, and where the estate of a citizen is concerned the treaty
has no application.[73]

It is to be noticed that the court was of the opinion that
national treatment provisions in treaties had no application
to estates left by citizens to nonresident aliens. The citizenship of the decedent was paramount in the court's consideration. No attention was given to the fact that such a decision
certainly deprived the heir of national treatment and of that
equality of treatment which the treaty attempted to achieve.

The Supreme Court of the State of Washington, many
years later, interpreted a similar treaty provision for the
benefit of the recipient rather than the deceased citizen. A
naturalized citizen of the United States left some property
to nonresident aliens, subjects of Norway. The state levied
the discriminatory tax upon the legacy, and the heir pro-

---

[72] Convention with Württemberg, Apr. 10, 1844, 8 *Stat.* 588.
[73] *Frederickson v. Louisiana* (1859), 23 How. 445.

tested that such a levy was in contravention of the treaty.[74] The court accepted the logic of this contention:

It is therefore apparent that the levy of a tax of this nature has the direct effect of impairing the right or privilege of receiving property by testament or inheritance; and in that manner this tax impairs the right of these appellants to take since it withholds from them 25 per cent. of the property they would be entitled to were they citizens of the United States and this law did not exist.[75]

The court went on to say that "to whatever extent the right or privilege of a citizen of the United States to take property by testament or inheritance is impaired by our own laws . . . to that extent will the rights of the citizens of Norway and Sweden be impaired without violating the terms of this treaty," but if an heir who is a citizen is taxed only three per centum while a nonresident alien, subject of Norway, is taxed at the rate of twenty-five per centum, such discrimination is a violation of the treaty under consideration.

It is suggested that of the two decisions discussed immediately above, the reasoning of the Supreme Court of the State of Washington is more consonant with the treaty provisions concerned. It appears that to interpret the provisions solely upon the basis of the citizenship of the decedent is to give only half an interpretation. A more correct interpretation would seem to necessitate some consideration for the recipient. It is to be noticed that both treaty provisions have these two stipulations which, although differently worded, have substantially the same meaning. The treaty with Württemberg provides: "and their heirs, legatees, and donees, *being citizens or subjects of the other contracting party,* shall succeed" to the property, "paying such duties only as *the inhabitants of the country where the*

[74] Treaty of July 4, 1827, 8 *Stat.* 346.
[75] *In re Stixrud's Estate* (1910), 109 Pac. (Wash.) 343.

said property lies, shall be liable to pay in like cases." The
treaty with Norway and Sweden makes a similar provision
for national treatment for "their heirs *in whatever place they
shall reside.*" [Italics mine.] But in most of the other cases
investigated, the court did not follow the reasoning of the
Washington court in cases where the deceased was a citizen
of the United States.

Seven years after the *Stixrud* case the United States Supreme Court had occasion to hear an appeal from the
Supreme Court of the State of Iowa. In this case the decedent was a citizen of the United States and the heirs were
nonresident aliens, subjects of Denmark. The heirs protested a discriminatory tax levied by the state on the ground
that it violated a national treatment provision in a treaty
with Denmark.[76]

After quoting Article VII of the treaty, Mr. Chief Justice White wrote:

We are constrained to this conclusion [that the treaty was in-
applicable] because the case here presented concerns only the
power of the State of Iowa to deal with a citizen of that State
and her property there situated, while the prohibitions of the
treaty, giving to them their widest significance, apply only to a
citizen of Denmark and his right to dispose of his property
situated in the State of Iowa. This is undoubted because there
is no controversy as to the first, the citizenship in Iowa, and
there is not room for substantial doubt as to the latter, since on
the face of the treaty the contractual limitations which it provides
are manifestly intended not to control or limit the right of either
of the governments to deal with its own citizens and their property within its borders, but were solely intended to restrict the
power of both of the governments to deal with citizens of the
other and their property within its dominions.[77]

Still placing the emphasis upon the citizenship of the deceased, the court pursued this reasoning:

[76] Treaty of 1857, 11 *Stat.* 719.
[77] *Petersen v. Iowa* (1917), 245 U. S. 170.

... the right of the citizens of each of the contracting countries reciprocally to own, dispose of or transmit their property situated in the other country, free from provisions or restrictions discriminating because of alienage, is in the largest possible sense that which is protected by the treaty. And conversely this being true, it follows also that the treaty did not protect the right of the citizens of either country to acquire by transfer or inheritance property situated in the other belonging to its own citizens free from the restraints imposed by the law of such country on its own citizens even although such restraints would not have been applicable in case the property had been disposed of or transmitted to a citizen.

It is necessary to mention one more phase of this opinion. It was maintained that the inheritance tax was a tax on the right to remove property and therefore, inasmuch as the tax rate was higher than that levied upon a citizen, there was a violation of national treatment in the right to remove property from the United States. The court answered this argument by holding that the tax was not such a burden because the alien's property right could not become vested in him until payment of the tax was made, because this right of property was dependent on that payment.

There is precedent for the idea that an inheritance tax is not *droit de détraction*.[78] But whether or not an inheritance tax and *droit de détraction* are the same is beside the point. The treaty specifically stipulates that no higher charges shall be levied on the removal of property *"upon the inheritance of such property, money, or effects,* or otherwise, than are or shall be payable in each State, upon the same when removed by a citizen or subject of each State respectively." [Italics mine.] In view of this last quotation from the treaty provision it is exceedingly difficult to go with the court in the statement that "it follows also that the treaty did not protect the right of the citizens of either country

[78] *In re Peterson's Estate* (1915), 151 N. W. (Iowa) 66; *In re Strobel's Estate* (1896), 39 N. Y. S. 169.

to acquire by *transfer or inheritance* property situated in the other belonging to its own citizens free from the restraints imposed by the law of such country on its own citizens even although such restraints would not have been applicable in case the property had been disposed of or transmitted to a citizen." [Italics mine.]

The court seems not only to place the emphasis of its reasoning upon the citizenship of the decedent, but also to indicate plainly that any interpretation of the provision, other than the one made in the court's opinion, would irresistibly bring one to the conclusion that the United States would have entered into a treaty which set limits upon the government's control of American citizens. Has not this court upheld other treaties placing limitations upon the control of American citizens? Can it be denied that any national treatment provision in a treaty is a limitation upon the contracting governments' control of their respective citizens or subjects? It is difficult to see how the court's interpretation has any other effect than that of rendering meaningless the words and spirit of the treaty provision.[79]

When the decedent is a resident alien, a different interpretation of these treaty provisions seems to be the law. However, even in the case of a resident alien decedent there is judicial opinion that discrimination in taxation of property going to nonresident aliens does not violate such treaty provisions. The Supreme Court of Iowa came to this conclusion

---

[79] Other opinions following the reasoning in *Petersen v. Iowa* are: *In re Anderson's Estate* (1914), 147 N. W. (Iowa) 1098; *In re Peterson's Estate* (1915), 151 N. W. (Iowa) 66, affirmed in *Duus v. Brown* (1917), 245 U. S. 176; *Moody v. Hagen* (1917), 162 N. W. (N. D.) 704, affirmed in *Skarderud v. Tax Commission* (1917), 245 U. S. 633.

There are several cases which express approval of the reasoning of the United States Supreme Court in *Petersen v. Iowa,* and declare the discrimination a violation of the treaty provision. This is because they are concerned with a treaty with Great Britain which specifically enumerates succession taxes among those in which discrimination is forbidden: *Trott v. State* (1919), 171 N. W. (N. D.) 827; *McKeown v. Brown* (1914), 149 N. W. (Iowa) 593; *In re Moynihan's Estate* (1915), 151 N. W. (Iowa) 504.

in *In re Petersen's Estate.*[80] The court's reasoning was that its decision in *In re Anderson's Estate*[81] had been upheld by the United States Supreme Court,[82] therefore:

> The question . . . is not an open one in this state. We have no disposition to depart from the rule announced in the Anderson Case . . . we now hold . . . an inheritance tax upon an estate to aliens who are residents of the kingdom of Denmark greater than is imposed upon citizens of the United States is not in contravention of the provisions of Article 7 of the treaty between the United States and the kingdom of Denmark.

But it is to be remembered that the cases upon which the court based its decision concern legacies left by *citizens.*

Another decision of the Supreme Court of Iowa involving a similar set of facts[83] was appealed to the United States Supreme Court. This case involved the applicability of Article VII of the treaty with Denmark of 1826 to property left by a resident alien to a nonresident alien. The United States Supreme Court interpreted the provision differently. Mr. Justice Stone, speaking for the court, pointed out: "the decedent was a citizen of Denmark, owning property within the state of Iowa, and Article 7, by its terms, is applicable to charges or taxes levied on personal property or effects of such a citizen; hence its protection may be invoked here if the discrimination complained of is one embraced within the terms of the Treaty."[84] And to the court: "the existence of discrimination was evident, since the tax is imposed only when the non-resident heirs are also aliens."

The most noteworthy development of this decision is that the court found that a discrimination existed by going against precedent and concluding that *droit de détraction* when used in treaties should be interpreted to include in-

[80] (1924), 196 N. W. (Iowa) 785.
[81] (1914), 147 N. W. (Iowa) 1098.   [82] *Petersen v. Iowa.*
[83] *In re Anderson's Estate* (1928), 218 N. W. (Iowa) 140.
[84] *Nielsen v. Johnson* (1929), 279 U. S. 47.

heritance taxes. Speaking of *droit de détraction,* the court said:

Its origin and an examination of the commentators likewise leave no doubt that the *droit de détraction*—the tax—accrued upon the death of the decedent, and only after it had been collected was the heir entitled to take possession of the property and remove or otherwise dispose of it. It was thus the precursor of the modern inheritance tax, differing from it in its essentials solely in that it was levied only where one of the parties to the inheritance was an alien or non-resident. . . .

That the present discriminatory tax is the substantial equivalent of the *droit de détraction* is not open to doubt. That it was the purpose of the high contracting parties to prohibit discriminatory taxes of this nature clearly appears from the diplomatic correspondence preceding and subsequent to the execution of the Treaty. . . .

It is true that the tax prohibited by the Treaty is in terms a tax on property or on its removal, but it is also true that the modern conception of an inheritance tax as a tax on the privilege of transmitting or succeeding to property of a decedent, rather than on the property itself, was probably unknown to the draftsmen of Article 7. But whatever, in point of present day legal theory, is the subject of the tax it is the property transmitted which pays it, as the Iowa statute carefully provides. In the face of the broad language embracing "charges, or taxes of any kind . . . upon the personal property . . . on the removal of the same . . . either upon the inheritance of such property . . . or otherwise," the omission, at that time, of words more specifically describing inheritance taxes as now defined, can hardly be deemed to evidence any intention not to include taxes theoretically levied upon the right to transmit or inherit, but which nevertheless were to be paid from the inheritance before it could be possessed or removed. Moreover, while it is true that the tax is levied whether the property is actually removed or not, it is nevertheless, imposed only with respect to a class of persons who would normally find it necessary so to remove the property in order to enjoy it, and since payment of the tax is a prerequisite to removal, the tax is, in its practical operation, one on removal. In the light of the avowed purpose of the Treaty to forbid discriminatory taxes of this character, and its use of language historically deemed to embrace them, such effect should be given to its provisions.

The contention that the present discrimination is not one forbidden by the language of Article 7, since the decedent's power of disposal is the same as that of a citizen, leaves out of consideration both the nature of the tax contemplated by the contracting parties and the fact that the treaty provisions extend explicitly to the withdrawal of such property by the alien heir upon inheritance and . . . protect him in his right to receive his inheritance undiminished by a tax which is not imposed upon citizens of the other contracting party.

This interpretation of the *droit de détraction* would seem to render invalid the argument that an inheritance tax is not a tax upon the removal of property, but merely a tax upon the right to transmit property. Moreover, it should be noticed that the United States Supreme Court placed the emphasis of its consideration not upon the citizenship of the decedent, but upon that of the recipient. True, it made mention of the fact that the decedent was a resident alien, but it is submitted that the whole emphasis of the decision was upon the recipient's right to receive the legacy undiminished by a discriminatory tax.

When the decedent was a citizen, the court considered primarily his citizenship as controlling, and held that such treaty provisions were not applicable. But when the decedent was a resident alien, it was held that the same treaty provisions were applicable. It is difficult to see any logical distinction here. It is suggested that the reasoning in *Nielsen v. Johnson,* which was extensively quoted above, is equally applicable for instance to the decision in *Petersen v. Iowa.*

Because of the presence of the Fourteenth Amendment in the United States Constitution, states are prohibited from levying any discriminatory taxes, other than greater charges for hunting licenses and such, against resident aliens. However, since the amendment does not extend beyond the territorial jurisdiction of the United States, states have successfully discriminated against nonresident aliens in the matter of inheritance taxes. It is believed, however, that treaty provisions stipulating equal treatment in the removal of inheritances from the United States by nonresident aliens would be more correctly interpreted should the courts place emphasis upon the recipient rather than upon the decedent. The reasoning in *Nielsen v. Johnson* seems to be an interpretation more consonant with the intention and purpose of such treaty provisions. Should this reasoning become law applicable to legacies left by both citizen and alien decedents, then the treaty provisions will have accomplished what seems their obvious purpose—that is, equal treatment for nonresidents of the United States as well as residents, which latter is assured by the Fourteenth Amendment to the United States Constitution.

V

ALIENS' RIGHT TO WORK

A GOVERNMENT which lays any claim to being civilized certainly must extend to all resident within its jurisdiction, alien or national, freedom of opportunity to engage in employment of some kind for the sustenance of the individual. The latitude of choice given aliens in this matter in the United States is a practical aspect of the general question of treatment accorded aliens.

The right of aliens to employment is to be discussed under the following headings: ordinary employment, employment on public works, employment in the exploitation of natural resources, and rights under workmen's compensation laws.

1. *Employment in ordinary occupations:*—It is a well-established and well-recognized principle in American jurisprudence that employment is property which is protected by all the constitutional guaranties extended to other forms of property. Inasmuch as it has the characteristic of property, one is immediately forced to realize that employment is placed in that category of possessions which has been traditionally one of the most carefully protected and jealously guarded by government in the United States. Therefore, it is to be expected that aliens should receive much freedom and protection in their employment.

However, to avoid giving the impression that there is no discrimination against aliens in the matter of employment, it should be made clear at this point that discrimination does exist and that aliens do not have as much freedom as nationals. In the exercise of their police power, states have discriminated against aliens.[1] Likewise, in public works and in the exploitation of natural resources legislative bodies, both national and state, have discriminated against aliens, and these discriminations have been upheld by the courts. It is suggested, however, that discrimination by governmental agencies which cannot be substantiated as a valid exercise of police power, or which is in no way connected with public works or natural resources, is illegal. In other words, while employed in what is here called ordinary economic activity, the alien stands upon a footing substantially the same as that of a national.

No consideration is to be given to the national legislation which has for its purpose the exclusion of Chinese labor. This subject matter is more directly concerned with the problem of immigration, which is beyond the scope of the present study. Here we are concerned only with the rights and privileges of aliens *after* they have gained legal entry into the United States.

Any consideration of the right of aliens to work must proceed from the well-known case of *Truax v. Raich.* This case involved an Arizona statute which required all business enterprises in that state employing more than five persons to have at least eighty per centum of their personnel composed of citizens of the United States. Mr. Justice Hughes, speaking for the court, in condemnation of the statute said:

It requires no argument to show that the right to work for a living in the *common* occupations of the community is of the very essence of the personal liberty and opportunity that it was the purpose of the [Fourteenth] Amendment to secure.

The discrimination is against aliens as such in competition with citizens in the described range of enterprises and in our

---

[1] F. V. Harper, "Due Process of Law in State Labor Legislation," 26 *Mich. Law Rev.* 599-630; 763-789; 888-905.

opinion it clearly falls under the condemnation of the fundamen
tal law.[2]

Some thirty years before the Arizona statute the legislature of California enacted a law in pursuance of a constitutional provision which had very much the same effect as
the Arizona statute. The California act prohibited corporations chartered by the state from employing Chinese subjects. Employment of such individuals was made a criminal
offense and the officers of the offending corporation were
liable to criminal action. In the case of *In re Tiburcio Par-
rott*[3] it was argued that the statute violated the treaty with
China of June 18, 1868. The treaty extended most-favored-
nation treatment in the matter of employment. It was
pointed out to the court that treaties with other nations
extended national treatment in the matter of employment,
and hence, it was argued, the most-favored-nation clause of
the Chinese treaty obtained the same right for Chinese.

The court admitted the correctness of this reasoning but
went further and held that such a statute violated not only
the treaty, but also the Fourteenth Amendment to the
United States Constitution. Judge Sawyer in his concurring
opinion maintained that labor is property and hence protected by the Fourteenth Amendment against improper
state legislation. It was his opinion that the "equal protection" and "due process" clauses of the amendment placed
the right of every *person* "upon the same secure footing and
under the same protection as are the rights of citizens themselves under other provisions of the constitution." Judge
Hoffman said that the amendment was sufficient reason for
declaring the California statute void, because "the corporations have a constitutional right to utilize their property
by employing such laborers as they choose, and on such
wages as may be mutually agreed upon; they are not com-

[2] (1915), 239 U. S. 33. Italics mine.   [3] (1880), 1 Fed. 481.

pelled to shelter themselves behind the treaty right of the Chinese, to reside here, to labor for their living, and accept employment when offered. . . ."

In 1897, Pennsylvania attempted to reduce the alien's opportunity for employment through its taxing power. The Pennsylvania Act of June 5, 1897, imposed upon every employer of foreign-born unnaturalized male persons over twenty-one years of age a tax of three cents a day for each day that they were employed. The act also authorized the employer to deduct the tax he had to pay from the wages paid the employee. This, too, was declared to be unconstitutional because the act was evidently "intended to hinder the employment of foreign-born unnaturalized male persons over twenty-one years of age" and, therefore, was prohibited by the Fourteenth Amendment.[4]

A second California statute, subsequent to the one referred to above, sought to infringe the freedom of aliens (specifically of Chinese) not by attempting to deny them the opportunity for employment, but by setting aside a district in San Francisco in which Chinese must live and carry on their trades and occupations. This law, likewise, was peremptorily declared unconstitutional. In the court's opinion it was not a valid exercise of the police power. In fact, Judge Sawyer stated with evident impatience:

The ordinance is not aimed at any particular vice, or any particular unwholesome or immoral occupation, or practice. . . . The obvious purpose of this order, is to drive out Chinese.

That this ordinance is a direct violation of not only the express provisions of the constitution of the United States, in several particulars, but also of the express provisions of our several treaties with China, and of the statutes of the United States, is so obvious, that I shall not waste more time, or words in discussing the matter.[5]

[4] *Fraser v. McConway* (1897), 82 Fed. 257. For state court decisions holding the same see *Ade v. County Commissioners* (1897), 7 Pa. Dist. 199; *Juniata Co. v. Blair County Commissioners* (1897), 7 Pa. Dist. 201.

[5] *In re Lee Sing* (1890), 43 Fed. 359.

In addition to attempting to restrict alien employment generally, statutes have sought, chiefly through the police power, to interfere with the alien in the pursuit of specific employments.

A Washington statute denied pawnbrokers' licenses to aliens. Only citizens of the United States were eligible for such licenses. A Japanese subject, resident in Seattle, pleaded that this law violated the United States Constitution and the treaty of April 5, 1911, with Japan. The treaty extended national treatment in "trade." The United States Supreme Court did not concern itself with the question of whether the law violated the plaintiff's rights under the Constitution, but based its decision upon the treaty. The court found that pawnbrokerage was a legitimate and normal activity included in the term "trade" and came to the conclusion that inasmuch as citizens could obtain licenses for pawnbrokerage, so could subjects of Japan resident in the United States.[6]

The privilege of operating a soft drink stand was extended by an Oregon statute only to citizens of the United States. The court, however, was unable to see how such regulation of soft drink stands could be associated with the police power. To the court it was just one of the many normal occupations, and being such, it could not be interfered with in this manner. In stating the plaintiff's right to operate such a place, the court said: "As to the matters involved in this litigation, aliens are entitled in Oregon to the same treatment accorded to native-born citizens. . . . In other words, they *of right* may apply for licenses to engage in the business of selling soft drinks in Portland on the same basis that a native American may apply."[7]

The right of an alien to obtain a hawker's or peddler's license has caused some difference of judicial opinion as to

[6] *Asakura v. Seattle* (1924), 265 U. S. 332.
[7] *George v. Portland* (1925), 235 Pac. (Ore.) 681. Italics mine.

whether the issuance of such licenses only to citizens of the United States was a valid exercise of the police power. In the case of *State v. Montgomery* the court said:

... we are compelled to conclude that a statute which forbids peddling except under a license, and which provides that citizens of the United States may be licensed, and that aliens shall not be, is denial of the "equal protection of the laws." It is an unconstitutional discrimination against aliens. It does more than impose unequal burdens and charges upon the alien. It absolutely denies him the privilege of an occupation open to citizens, which is more than a discrimination in burdens. It does not permit the alien within our jurisdiction to pursue a business occupation and to acquire and enjoy property on equal terms with the citizen.[8]

Judge Savage, from whose opinion the above quotation is made, denied that such a statute could be considered a police measure, because the discrimination was not against a class "disqualified by character or habits, or as harmful to society, but against a class solely as aliens."

A similar hawker's license statute was upheld in Massachusetts.[9] Judge Savage's opinion in *State v. Montgomery* was cited to the Massachusetts court, but that court would not accept that interpretation of the police power. Mr. Chief Justice Knowlton, speaking for the court, said of the opinion in *State v. Montgomery*: "There is, however, an important question which was not much discussed in that case, Whether the Legislature, in the exercise of the police power, could discover a reason for withholding peddlers' licenses from aliens. The business of peddling furnishes such opportunities for the practice of fraud that it is a proper subject for legislative regulation."

The court preferred to follow the opinion in *Trageser v. Gray*,[10] which was based, as will be shown below, upon the premise that citizens of the United States are naturally more

---

[8] (1900), 47 Atl. (Me.) 165.
[9] *Commonwealth v. Hana* (1907), 195 Mass. 262.   [10] (1890), 73 Md. 250.

concerned with the welfare of social conditions in this country, and, therefore, less liable to commit abuses. The decision in *Commonwealth v. Hana* is based upon the assumption that peddling is replete with opportunities for fraud, and it is implied that aliens are more likely to take advantage of these opportunities than citizens. The court was "of opinion that the Legislature, in the exercise of the police power might make this requirement as to the qualifications of applicants for a peddler's license."

The case of *Trageser v. Gray* resulted from a Maryland statute which permitted only citizens of the United States to obtain retail liquor licenses. The Maryland court was of the opinion that this was a valid police measure. "The privilege is very liable to be abused, and abuses would produce great public detriment. It therefore seemed wise to the legislature to confer it only on those who, being [citizens] of the country, might reasonably be supposed to have a regard for its welfare. . . ."

Very much the same idea was expressed by the United States Supreme Court in a case involving a Cincinnati ordinance which denied licenses to operate poolrooms to aliens. This ordinance was claimed to be a violation of a treaty and of the Fourteenth Amendment. The treaty in question was that with Great Britain of 1827 which extended reciprocal liberty of commerce. The court was unable to see any necessary connection between "commerce" as used in the treaty and the operation of poolrooms. In answer to the plea that the ordinance violated the Fourteenth Amendment, the court agreed with the fact expressed in the title of the ordinance that poolrooms were a very possible source of antisocial activity. Citizen proprietors were less likely than alien proprietors to permit their establishments to become social menaces. The ordinance was upheld as an exercise of the police power and as no violation of any treaty rights.[11]

[11] *Clarke v. Deckebach* (1927), 274 U. S. 392.

It should be mentioned that three years before a lower federal court had upheld an Oregon statute regulating pool-rooms in the same way as did the Cincinnati ordinance. Judge Wolverton said:

. . . it is natural and reasonable to suppose that the foreign born, whose allegiance is first to their own country, and whose ideals of governmental environment and control have been engendered and formed under entirely different regimes and political sys-tems, have not the same inspiration for the public weal, nor are they as well disposed toward the United States, as those who, by citizenship, are a part of the government itself.[12]

The Michigan legislature attempted to discriminate against aliens in the matter of barbers' licenses by denying a license to anyone who, at the time of application, was an alien. The plaintiff pleaded that such a law was a violation of the Fourteenth Amendment. Counsel for the Board of Examiners cited the case of *Trageser v. Gray* in an effort to convince the court that such discrimination against aliens in the matter of barbers' licenses was a police measure. The court would not agree with this. It was said:

In that case the question presented was whether aliens could be excluded from engaging in the business of retailing liquors. This is a business peculiar to itself, which might be wholly pro-hibited by the legislature, and licenses might be conferred to a limited number. We need not, therefore, inquire whether such legislation is an infraction of the rights of the individual, not a citizen. But in the present case the relator's business is in no way injurious to the morals, the health, or even the convenience of the community, provided only he has the requisite knowledge upon the subjects prescribed by the legislature to practice his calling without endangering the health of his patrons. To hold that he is not entitled to practice this calling, because not a full citizen of the United States, is to deny him rights which we think are preserved by the Fourteenth Amendment.[18]

[12] *Anton v. Van Winkle* (1924), 297 Fed. 340.
[18] *Templar v. Board of Examiners* (1902), 131 Mich. 254.

The operation of a laundry is another specific occupation that has been singled out by states for legislation discriminating against aliens. A denial of the power of the legislature to attempt such discrimination on the basis of an exercise of the police power was made in the well-known case, *Yick Wo v. Hopkins*.[14]

The statute in question in this case required that persons wishing to operate laundries must obtain a license from a board of supervisors. The act gave the board full power to grant or withhold licenses as they saw fit. The facts of the case showed that the plaintiff was denied a license solely because of the fact that he was a Chinaman. The court was of the opinion that:

These provisions [Fourteenth Amendment] are universal in their application, to all persons within the territorial jurisdiction, without regard to any differences of race, color, or of nationality; and the equal protection of the laws is a pledge of the protection of equal laws.

It appears that both petitioners have complied with every requisite deemed by the law or by the public officers charged with its administration, necessary for the protection of neighboring property from fire, or as a precaution against injury to the public health. No reason whatever except the will of the supervisors is assigned why they should not be permitted to carry on, in the accustomed manner their harmless and useful occupation, on which they depend for a livelihood. . . . The discrimination is therefore, illegal, and the public administration which enforces it is a denial of the equal protection of the laws and a violation of the Fourteenth Amendment of the Constitution.

The legislature of Montana attempted to outlaw laundries operated by Chinese by an exercise of its taxing power. The statute levied a higher tax on laundries not operated by steam. This statute was also held to be a denial of the equal protection of the laws and hence prohibited by the Fourteenth Amendment.[15]

[14] (1886), 118 U. S. 356.   [15] *In re Yot Sang* (1896), 75 Fed. 983.

The New York court declared void a New York City ordinance which prohibited an alien from conducting an immigrant lodging house, because "there is nothing about the conduct of a general lodging house which differentiates it from an immigrant lodging house in the manner of conduct thereof or as a source of greater evils, if any, to be apprehended therefrom."[16]

In an obiter dictum, a federal court has said that a "state would have no power to exclude the individual underwriters from doing insurance business within its borders." The court was referring to alien individuals doing an insurance business. The case concerned the right of an insurance *corporation* to carry on business in a state. In this case, Judge Manton made this very suggestive statement: "Under article 4, §2, of the federal Constitution, *individuals* are entitled to all the privileges and immunities of the citizens of the several states."[17]

2. *Employment of aliens on public works:*—Discrimination against aliens in employment on public works has been made by both state and national legislatures. In many cases this discrimination has been sustained and held not to be a violation of the alien's rights. The theory which is the basis of the decisions sustaining such legislation is that when a state or municipality is constructing public works it is acting in the same capacity as private individuals, with the same rights that are enjoyed by them in their proprietary relations. However, there are some decisions holding that any such discrimination is a violation of the alien's rights. Inasmuch as the weight of authority seems to be to the contrary, it is proposed first to discuss those decisions sustaining discrimination against aliens.

[16] *Carvallo v. Cooper* (1930), 239 N. Y. S. 436.
[17] *Bobe v. Lloyds* (1926), 10 Fed. (2d) 730. Italics mine. It is not clear why such a statement should appear in the case. Taken alone the statement is patently incorrect. The constitutional provision specifically uses the term "citizens" and it is well established that it applies only to citizens. See R. Howell, *The Privileges and Immunities of State Citizenship.*

The case of *Heim v. McCall*[18] involved a New York statute which prohibited the employment of aliens on public works in that state. The United States Supreme Court denied that this legislation contravened an alien's rights under the constitution. The case of *Atkin v. Kansas*[19] was quoted with approval in that "it belongs to the State, as guardian and trustee for its people, and having control of its affairs, to prescribe the conditions upon which it will permit public works to be done on its behalf or on behalf of its municipalities."

In this case the treaty with Italy of 1871 was also cited to the court as a reason why the statute should be declared void. The treaty extended national treatment in employment. In answer to this contention the United States Supreme Court approvingly quoted the New York court from which the case was appealed. It was said that although the treaty did extend to Italians the right to employment upon the same basis as that enjoyed by nationals, it did not "limit the power of the State, *as a proprietor,* to control the construction of *its own works* and the distribution of *its own moneys.*" [Italics mine.]

A New York court stating the law relative to this type of statute said:

. . . the law appears to be that while a state or Congress may not legislate against any particular class of individuals, as to the general business they may pursue in this country, they may . . . in the conduct of their own business provide that only certain classes of laborers shall be employed without any violation of the Constitution or of treaty rights.

No State can deprive any person of his right . . . to labor for others; but a state, like an individual, may determine whom it will employ in the construction of its public works, and it is, like an individual, under no obligation to employ any class of laborers unless it desires so to do.[20]

[18] (1915), 239 U. S. 175. See also *Crane v. N. Y.* (1915), 239 U. S. 195.
[19] (1903), 191 U. S. 207.
[20] *People v. I. M. Ludington's Sons* (1911), 131 N. Y. S. 550.

Virtually the same interpretation of the law was made by another state court. A Massachusetts statute gave preference to citizens in obtaining employees for public works and public positions generally. Mr. Chief Justice Rugg said:

In its representative capacity, within appropriate functions of legislation, the general court stands in the position of employer. It may establish general rules for the employment of labor.

Where a state, either directly or through its governmental departments, acts as proprietor or employer, a determination not to engage aliens in its service cannot be pronounced unreasonable or violative of any constitutional mandate.[21]

As stated above, there have been decisions to the contrary. The validity of an Oregon statute was tested in a lower federal court. Anyone obtaining a contract for public work from the state was forbidden by the statute to employ Chinese on that work. The decision in the case of *Baker v. Portland*[22] was based upon a treaty with China rather than upon the Constitution. The court held that "the state cannot legislate so as to interfere with the operation of this treaty or limit or deny the privileges or immunities [one of which was residence] guaranteed by it to the Chinese residents in this country." The opinion went on to say that if the state could prevent Chinese obtaining this type of employment it could prevent their working at anything in that state. The treaty "impliedly recognizes their right to make this country their home, and expressly permits them to become permanent residents here; and this necessarily implies the right to live and to labor for a living."

Judge Deady's reasoning in *Baker v. Portland* was that the treaty, by giving the Chinese the right permanently to reside here, implied the right to labor for a living. However, he made no distinction as to public works and other types of employment. To him the implied right to earn a

---

[21] *Lee v. City of Lynn* (1916), 223 Mass. 109.
[22] (1879), Fed. Cas. 777.

living included laboring in public works as well as in other types of work. But it should be remembered that the United States Supreme Court in *Heim v. McCall* did make a distinction between public works and other forms of employment, and it was upon the basis of this distinction that a similar New York statute was declared not to be unconstitutional or violative of treaty rights.

A case was decided in Illinois which indirectly concerned an alien's right to labor on public works. A statute of the state permitted only the employment of citizens. A taxpayer (the opinion does not say whether he was a citizen or alien) contested the validity of a tax assessment made for a public improvement. He contended that the law provided that the bidders for the contract for the public work must agree to work their personnel only eight hours and to use only citizen labor. The plaintiff said that such restrictions as these two increased the cost of the improvement (and hence increased his tax bill) because the restrictions prevented several contractors from bidding. The court agreed with this and declared such restrictions upon contractors void because: "It is public policy to get the work done as cheaply as possible."[23]

Judge Ricks in an opinion upon the same statute likewise pronounced the placing of such restrictions upon bidders as being "in contravention of the Constitution and the right of individuals to contract."[24]

A California statute placed the state's road building program under the direction of a highway commission. The commission, on its own authority, issued a regulation that no contractor would be given any of the road construction unless he agreed to employ only citizens. Attention is directed to the fact that the exclusion of aliens was the *commission's* regulation.

[23] *Glover v. People* (1903), 201 Ill. 545.
[24] *Chicago v. Hulbert* (1903), 68 N. E. (Ill.) 786.

The court condemned the commission for making such a regulation upon its own initiative. Judge Shaw, speaking for the court, said:

> The statute in question charges the supervisors with the duty of administering the scheme for building roads, but it does not purport to confer power to make or enforce a provision of this character.

> No express authority for such a provision is given, and we are satisfied that the supervisors have no implied power to impose such a mischievous and burdensome restriction.[25]

What the court would have held, had the statute given this authority to the commission, is another question.

All the cases relative to employment of aliens on public works which have been considered have involved state legislation. There is also federal public works legislation which discriminates against aliens.[26] Only one case concerning the exclusion of aliens from employment on such works has been found.

Rok brought an action against Legg, administrator of the W. P. A. for southern California, on the grounds that Legg was discriminating against him because of the alienage of the plaintiff. Rok argued that exclusion of aliens violated the "due process" clause of the Fifth Amendment. In the opinion, Judge Yankwich took the position that W. P. A. employment was in the nature of a bounty. He said that the guarantee of due process in the Fifth Amendment is not broader than the similar guarantee in the Fourteenth Amendment for this purpose. Therefore, "if a state, in creating public work either as a means of alleviating poverty

---

[25] *City Street Improvement Co. v. Kroh* (1910), 158 Cal. 308.

[26] For example, Act of 1902, 32 *Stat.* 388, sec. 4, prohibits employment of Mongolians on United States reclamation projects. The Treasury and Post Office Appropriation Act of 1939, 75 Cong., 3 Sess., Pub. Act 453, sec. 5, provides that money hereby appropriated can be used to employ only citizens of the United States or aliens who have declared their intention to become citizens. The Emergency Relief Appropriations Act of 1938, as amended, 53 *Stat.* 508, sec. 11, prohibits the employment of aliens on W. P. A. projects.

or relieving unemployment may give preference to citizens, it is difficult to see why the federal government may not do so." The court went on to say: "Once legally in the United States, and so long as he does not violate its laws, the alien is accorded the same protection against arbitrary power as the citizen. If he is denied the *privilege* of sharing in the *bounty* of the government through employment on public works, the fault lies at his own door" for coming to the United States.[27] In arriving at the decision the court relied upon cases involving state discrimination in the matter of employment of aliens on public works.

3. *Employment of aliens in the exploitation of the public domain:*—The first case to be considered in this connection is one which does not concern an alien. Nevertheless, it is believed that consideration is necessary because it lays the foundation for the idea that the state is a trustee for its citizens and that any regulation it makes concerning public domain is an exercise of this trusteeship. The fisheries, mines, and other natural resources are property owned jointly by the citizens of the state, and they have intrusted the care of the domain to the state.

A Virginia statute restricted the enjoyment of the right of fishing within the navigable waters of the state to citizens of Virginia. A citizen of Maryland was arrested for violating the law. He carried his case to the United States Supreme Court on the ground that the state was prohibited by the "privileges and immunities" clause of the Fourteenth Amendment to the United States Constitution from excluding him from the fisheries. Mr. Chief Justice Waite, speaking for the court, said:

The principle has long been settled in this court, that each State owns the beds of all tide-waters within its jurisdiction, unless they have been granted away. . . . In like manner, the State owns the tide-waters themselves, and the fish in them, so

---

[27] *Rok v. Legg* (1939), 27 Fed. Supp. 243. Italics mine.

far as they are capable of ownership while running. For this purpose the State represents its people, and the ownership is that of the people in their united sovereignty. . . . The title thus held is subject to the paramount right of navigation, the regulation of which, in respect to foreign and inter-state commerce, has been granted to the United States. There has been, however, no such grant of power over fisheries. These remain under the exclusive control of the State, which has consequently the right, in its discretion, to appropriate its tide-waters and their beds to be used by its people as a common for taking and cultivating fish, so far as it may be done without obstructing navigation. Such an appropriation is in effect nothing more than a regulation of the use by the people of their common property. The right which the people of the State thus acquired comes not from their citizenship alone, but from their citizenship and property combined. It is, in fact a property right, and not a mere privilege or immunity of citizenship.[28]

The legislative assembly of Rhode Island enacted a statute which gave a commission discretionary powers in granting fishing licenses. Several aliens who made their living by lobster fishing were arrested and penalized for fishing without a license. They pleaded that such a statute was void because of the Fourteenth Amendment. The court, however, considered it a valid exercise of the police power and a measure for the protection of fisheries which are the common property of the citizens of Rhode Island.[29]

In his dissenting opinion, Judge Blodgett rather cogently reasoned that it was a denial of due process to permit the *commissioners* to refuse licenses to aliens because they were aliens. He pointed out that giving such great powers to administrative officers was a practice severely condemned by the United States Supreme Court in *Yick Wo v. Hopkins.*

It would seem that although a state may discriminate against aliens *as a class* in the public domain, it may not con-

[28] *McCready v. Virginia* (1876), 94 U. S. 391.
[29] *State v. Kofines* (1911), 33 R. I. 211.

stitutionally discriminate against a certain race or group of aliens.[80] A California statute denied the privilege of fishing in California waters to all who were ineligible to become electors. This, of course, was directed chiefly against Mongolians. In declaring the law void Judge Sawyer of the Federal Circuit Court said:

> The fourteenth amendment of the national constitution provides that "no state shall . . . deny to *any person* within its jurisdiction the equal protection of the laws." To subject the Chinese to imprisonment for fishing in the waters of the state, while aliens of all European nations under the same circumstances are exempt from any punishment whatever, is to subject the Chinese to other and entirely different punishments, pains and penalties than those to which others are subjected, and it is to deny them the equal protection of the laws contrary to those provisions of the constitution.[81]

A license statute was enacted by the Florida legislature which discriminated against aliens who removed oysters "for other than their own use." This was upheld on this basis:

> The state may, without denying "to any person within its jurisdiction the equal protection of the laws," justly discriminate in favor of its citizens in regulating the taking for private use of the common property in fish and oysters found in the public waters of the state, where such regulations have a fair relation to and are suited to conserve the common rights which the citizens of the state have in such fish and oysters as against aliens and nonresidents of the state. The equal rights of all persons who reside in a state whether citizens or aliens to labor therein does not include an equal right of an alien to participate in the common property and privileges that are peculiar to citizens. The statute does not purport to discriminate against aliens and nonresidents with reference to private property rights or the

[80] See Note, "Constitutionality of Legislative Discrimination Against the Alien in His Right to Work," 83 *Univ. of Pa. Law Rev.* 74-82.

[81] *In re Ah Chong* (1880), 2 Fed. 733.

right to labor or to deal in fish and oysters after they lawfully become private property.[32]

A California statute requiring the payment of a certain sum of money by aliens for working gold mines in that state was sustained.[33]

Congress has exercised a like power over the public domain of the United States. The Act of June 14, 1906,[34] permits only citizens and those who have declared their intention of becoming citizens to take fish from Alaskan waters by means other than "rod, spear, or gaff." In other words, there is a discrimination in the right to engage in commercial fishing. It is pertinent to note that the law stipulates:

That nothing contained in this Act shall prevent any person, firm, corporation, or association lawfully entitled to fish in the waters of Alaska from employing as laborers any aliens who can *now* be lawfully employed under the existing law of the United States, either at stated wages or by piecework, or both, in connection with Alaskan fisheries, or with the canning, salting or otherwise preserving of fish. [Italics mine.]

This act was upheld in the case of the *Tokai Maru*.[35]

No better summary of the law on the alien's right to work could be made than by quoting from Judge Wolverton's opinion in *Anton v. Van Winkle:*

Plaintiff, [an alien] along with citizens of the United States, has the right to work and so employ himself as to gain a livelihood. Primarily, he has the same right and privilege as citizens under similar conditions to engage in useful gainful employment and occupations, unless they pertain to the regulation or distribution of the public domain, or to the common property or resources of the people of the State . . . or pertain to public works or benefits to be received from public moneys.[36]

---

[32] *Ex parte Gilletti* (1915), 70 Fla. 442.
[33] *People v. Naglee* (1850), 1 Cal. 232.
[34] 34 *Stat.* 263, sec. 1.
[35] (1911), 190 Fed. 450.   [36] (1924), 297 Fed. 340.

4. *Rights of aliens under the workmen's compensation laws of the several states:*—Aliens, resident in the United States, receive national treatment under the workmen's compensation laws that are in force in the several states. No statute has been found in which alien employees have been excluded from the provisions of these laws, nor has any been found which attempts to give unequal treatment to beneficiaries who are resident aliens. It is believed that any attempt on the part of state legislatures to bring about unequal treatment for resident aliens would be a violation of the Fourteenth Amendment to the United States Constitution. Only one case can be invoked to support this position.

A Kansas statute was interpreted by the commission so as to make the limit of compensation for nonresident aliens, which was $750, applicable to resident aliens. This was done by taking some liberties with rather unique phraseology. The beneficiary, a resident alien, feeling that the law gave such aliens national treatment, appealed to the courts.[37]

The court not only disagreed with the commission's interpretation, but went further to say that an interpretation which has the effect of discriminating against resident aliens was a violation of the Fourteenth Amendment. In support of his position, the Chief Justice relied upon the case of *Truax v. Raich.*

The *Vietti* case is the only one that has been found dealing directly with the problem of the rights of resident alien beneficiaries. Of course it is not overwhelming judicial opinion. Moreover, the basis for the position taken by the court was a case which had to do with an alien's right to engage in the ordinary ways of making a living. Nevertheless, it is believed that the position is sound. One of the purposes of the compensation laws is to create a situation whereby the dependents of workingmen may obtain assistance to prevent, or to lessen the likelihood of, their becoming public

[37] *Vietti v. Mackie Fuel Co.* (1921), 197 Pac. (Kan.) 881.

charges. It is difficult to accept a position which would seek to sustain unequal treatment in this respect upon the grounds that it was a reasonable classification for purposes of state police power.[38]

Since the United States Supreme Court and many state courts have established the principle in American jurisprudence that aliens have the right to ordinary employment, it seems to follow naturally that the same "equal protection of the laws" assures them the right to participate upon an equal basis in the benefits of the workmen's compensation laws. More especially does this seem true in view of the purpose of these laws as stated above. The case of *Vietti v. Mackie Fuel Co.,* taken in conjunction with the purpose of the laws, the lack of litigation upon the subject, the absence of discrimination against resident aliens in the provisions of various state statutes would seem to justify and support the belief that, so far as resident aliens are concerned, compensation laws may make no discrimination between them and citizens.

When the rights of nonresident aliens are considered, discrimination is found. It is well established that such persons are not protected by the Fourteenth Amendment. In states which discriminate against such aliens, the discrimination takes several forms.[39] Some of them give compensation to certain relatives whether they are citizens, residents, or nonresident aliens. But in the case of nonresident aliens, the law permits them to receive only a stipulated percentage of the amount which would have gone to that relative had he been a resident of the state. Other states, instead of using the percentage limitation, provide that compensation shall not exceed a stipulated amount of money. A third group of states not only limits the amount receivable by a nonresident alien beneficiary by means of a percentage

[38] T. R. Powell, "The Workmen's Compensation Cases," 32 *Pol. Sci. Quar.* 542-569; E. H. Downey, *Workmen's Compensation.*
[39] See below, Appendix C (b).

or stipulated sum, but places a further limitation upon such aliens in the classification of relatives to whom such compensation may be paid. These statutes provide in substance that the term "dependents" when used in connection with payments to nonresident aliens shall be confined to a more limited number of relatives, usually to spouse, children, and sometimes parents. A few statutes have the additional stipulation based upon the idea of reciprocal treatment, whereby it is provided that if the country of which the nonresident alien is a citizen should deny similar treatment to citizens of the United States, the compensation which would ordinarily go to such dependents is to be denied them and turned over to the state fund.

A second group of statutes extends equal treatment to nonresident alien beneficiaries.[40] However, there is to be found some discrimination. In other words, there are several statutes which do not extend equal treatment to nonresident aliens generally, but only to certain classes, extending national treatment to widows, children, and sometimes parents, but denying compensation to any other relatives.

Naturally a statute providing compensation for nonresident aliens has been contested on the ground that it was a violation of the Fourteenth Amendment to require the payment of compensation to such beneficiaries. But the United States Supreme Court could not agree that such a provision violated the "due process" clause of the amendment. Mr. Justice Sanford, speaking for the court, said:

If an employment be such as to fall within the State lawmaking jurisdiction and the legislature determines that the employment of labor therein entails upon the employer certain responsibilities toward the persons performing the labor and those dependent upon them, there is no constitutional provision requiring that the benefits of such legislative scheme be limited to citizens or residents of the State.[41]

[40] Ibid., (c).
[41] Madera Sugar Pine Co. v. Industrial Accident Commission (1923), 262 U. S. 499.

Likewise, it is to be expected that nonresident alien beneficiaries should contest the validity of statutes which refuse them compensation or grant only a part of the amount given to residents. An early New Jersey statute denied compensation to all nonresident alien beneficiaries. Mr. Justice Trenchard of that state said "that the power of the Legislature . . . to declare to whom and in what amount compensation shall be made can not be doubted."[42]

Under a Kentucky statute, a nonresident alien received only one half the compensation awarded to a resident. It was argued that such discrimination was in conflict with the Fourteenth Amendment. The court denied that any such conflict existed, on the ground that the alien was not "a person within its jurisdiction" and therefore, such a provision could not violate the amendment.[43]

There seems to be no doubt of the fact that, so far as nonresident aliens are concerned, there is no constitutional obstacle to a state's denying compensation to such aliens, or allowing them only a part of that allowed to residents. There are many cases supporting this position. The two used immediately above have been rather arbitrarily chosen. However, no case has been found which throws any doubt upon the validity of the opinion that states are not constitutionally bound to extend equal treatment to nonresident aliens.

Only three states deny nonresident aliens any compensation.[44] All other states give compensation of one kind or another. The fact that most of the states discriminate in one way or another may seem to some an undesirable condition. It may be felt that the employee with nonresident alien dependents is not treated equally with the employee whose dependents are resident in the United States. With this premise one could, without much difficulty, come to the

[42] *Gregutis v. Waclark Wire Works* (1914), 92 Atl. (N. J.) 354.

[43] *Maryland Casualty Co. v. Chamos* (1924), 263 S. W. (Ky.) 370.

[44] Alabama, New Mexico, and South Dakota.

conclusion that such statutes are an unconstitutional discrimination against employees. Be that as it may, the courts have looked at the statutes from the viewpoint of the beneficiaries and not the employees. Moreover, it must be kept in mind that one of the very important reasons for workmen's compensation laws is to reduce the possibility of increasing public charges through industrial accidents. That the nonresident alien beneficiary is likely to become a public charge on the state is a remote contingency.

Treaties, of course, could alter such discriminatory legislation. No instance has been found where any of the existing treaties has altered the provisions concerning nonresident alien beneficiaries in any of the compensation laws. There have been cases in which it was pleaded that discrimination was a violation of treaty rights. But the courts have looked upon the compensation laws as involving a voluntary and contractual relationship entered into by the employer and employee. Therefore, if the employee enters into this relationship, his beneficiaries cannot plead a treaty in order to alter this contractual situation.[45] It is possible that at some future date treaty provisions will appear, the phraseology of which would make such an interpretation impossible. However, at the present time such provisions do not exist.

There remains one other type of discrimination which must be mentioned. In Oregon, appeals from the findings of the Industrial Accident Commission lie in the circuit court functioning in the county where the appellee resides. Obviously this excludes nonresident aliens from the right of appeal from the commission. This was contested by a nonresident alien beneficiary on the ground that it violated the "privileges and immunities" clause of Article IV and the "equal protection" clause of the Fourteenth Amendment to the United States Constitution. The court could not see

[45] *Liberato v. Royer* (1926), 270 U. S. 535; *Norella v. Maryland Casualty Co.* (1926), 287 S. W. (Ky.) 18; *Madonna v. Wheeling Steel Co.* (1928), 28 Fed. (2d) 710.

how such provisions were violated, since the plaintiff was neither a citizen nor within the jurisdiction of the state. Mr. Justice Burnett said:

> To this purely statutory scheme for the financial betterment of the injured workman or his dependents, the Legislative Assembly had a right to append such conditions as it chose. It could provide a remedy by appeal for a resident of the state and leave out of that benefit the residents of foreign countries. . . . The state is under no obligation to provide largess for nonresident aliens, and may limit their access to its courts to narrower bounds than those accorded to its residents.[46]

5. *Summarizing statement:*—It is a principle of the American legal system that aliens legally within the United States have a right to engage in gainful employment. This right is guaranteed by the United States Constitution. The right, however, is subject to certain limitations. An alien is given an opportunity equal to that of a citizen in what may be termed the ordinary pursuits of life. He may legally be discriminated against in opportunities to obtain employment in public works. In this type of activity the courts assimilate the national, state, and municipal governments to private corporations or individuals, grant the governments the same latitude in employing whom they wish, and recognize their right to refuse employment to any that they wish. A second discrimination is found in the exploitation of natural resources. Here the courts consider the government as a trustee for the common property of the citizens of the particular state. In its capacity as trustee the government is speaking for the owners of this common property when it refuses or grants aliens the opportunity to such employment. Finally, aliens are denied the exercise of certain trades and professions on the ground that such vocations are peculiarly subject to the possibility of abuse, and there-

---

[46] *Liimatainen v. State Industrial Accident Commission* (1926), 246 Pac. (Ore.) 741.

fore a citizen, being naturally more interested in the welfare of the community, is less likely to resort to such abuses. That is to say, the state in denying aliens the right to pursue these vocations is exercising what in the court's mind is a valid police measure.

There is no discrimination between citizens and *resident* aliens in the matter of workmen's compensation legislation. Resident alien employees may not be denied the right to enjoy this type of insurance. Resident alien beneficiaries may not be discriminated against in the benefits resulting from such legislation. Where discrimination does sometimes exist it is in the payment of benefits to dependents who are nonresident aliens.[47]

[47] Legislation discriminating against nonresident alien beneficiaries is usually upheld by the courts; see Note, "Workmen's Compensation," 11 *Minn. Law Review* 57-65.

VI

ALIENS IN AMERICAN COURTS

THERE ARE remarkably few cases involving the alien's right of access to courts. The United States constitutional provisions on this subject employ the term "persons" thereby doing much to prevent litigation to determine whether or not an alien has access to American courts. The alien may as of right enter the courts, prosecute his case, and obtain protection of life, liberty, and property in as full and ample a manner as a citizen. The right is a constitutional one. This aspect of an alien's rights in American courts does not present enough controversial material to justify consideration in a study having to do with a comparison of the rights of aliens and citizens. Therefore, it is believed to be justifiable and proper merely to point out, without delving into the obvious, that equality of treatment does exist in this aspect of rights in courts.

Service on a jury in this country cannot be claimed as a right by resident aliens. Moreover, a citizen can make no such claim merely because of his citizenship. States are free to provide that jurors shall have qualifications other than citizenship; anyone failing to meet with these requirements is excluded from jury service and is unable to offer any legal reason why he should not be so excluded. However, in making qualifications, a state may not discriminate against any class of citizens solely because of their race.[1]

[1] See *In re Shibuya Jugiro* (1891), 140 U. S. 291; and *State v. Ah Chew* (1881), 16 Nev. 50.

In a great majority of states one of the qualifications for jurors is citizenship. Such a qualification automatically excludes aliens from jury service in most states.[2] The same is true in most of the United States courts. This is due to the fact that "jurors to serve in the courts of the United States respectively shall have the same qualifications . . . as jurors of the highest court of law in such State. . . ."[3] Therefore, in states requiring citizenship as one of the qualifications for jurors, the federal courts therein are likewise limited by the state's requirements, and no person who is not a citizen may serve on a jury in a federal court sitting in that state.

Although not directly a part of a discussion of an alien's present position relative to jury trial, the right to a jury de medietate linguae is of some historical interest. Under English law an alien was entitled to be tried by a jury composed of one half subjects of that country and one half aliens residing in the jurisdiction in which the trial was to take place. This form of jury trial was inaugurated during the reign of Edward III and was amended from time to time. Its purpose was to encourage the coming of aliens to England in order to stimulate commercial enterprise.[4]

There has been some difference of judicial opinion in our earlier history as to whether or not this right was part of the law inherited from England by the several states. In certain jurisdictions an alien's right to be tried by a jury de medietate linguae was recognized as having been part of the law inherited from England,[5] while in other jurisdictions it was not so considered.[6]

---

[2] See below, Appendix D.   [3] U. S. C. A., Tit. 28, sec. 411.

[4] For a brief but excellent summary of the purposes and nature of such legislation in England see Judge Duncan's opinion in *Richards v. Commonwealth* (1841), 11 Leigh (Va.) 690.

[5] *Respublica v. Mesca* (1783), 1 Dall. (Pa.) 73; *People v. McLean* (1807), 2 Johns. (N. Y.) 381; *Richards v. Commonwealth* (1841).

[6] *U. S. v. McMahon* (1835), Fed. Cas. 15,699; *State v. Antonio* (1825), 11 N. C. 200; *State v. Fuentes* (1850), 5 La. Ann. 427; *People v. Chin Mook Sow* (1877), 51 Cal. 597.

The reason for the nonrecognition of the validity of the principle in this country was expressed by Mr. Justice Hall in the following manner:

And if the statutes we are now considering were suitable and profitable for the government and well being of the colonies at that time, and even not afterwards repugnant to or inconsistent with the freedom and independence of the state and form of government therein established, I admit they are in force at this time. But it seems to me that those statutes were in their nature local; they were founded more in commercial policy than in general principles calculated to answer alone the ends of justice and reach the objects of criminal law.[7]

The English statute providing for such juries created a contradictory situation in English law. Under the common law an alien was ineligible to serve on a jury.[8] However, the statute under consideration created a contradictory situation by giving an alien the right to be tried by a jury one half of whom were aliens. If the common law were followed, one half of the jury were not qualified to function as jurors. While, on the other hand, if the statute were followed, one half of the jury were functioning in violation of the common law. It is true, of course, that in England, just as it is in this country, a subsequent statute modifies the common law. To be sure, this was no problem for the English courts. For their purposes the common law was modified by the statute, and when an alien came up for trial his jury was composed one half of aliens.

Nevertheless, it does create in this country a problem which in modern times may be more academic than anything else. In a few states[9] citizenship is not specifically stated as a qualification for a juror. Is alienage a bar to service on a jury in these states? If the common law is followed, an alien may not serve on a jury in these jurisdic-

---

[7] *State v. Antonio.*

[8] *Hinton v. Hinton* (1928), 196 N. C. 341. See also 1 *R. C. L.* 802.

[9] Illinois, Maryland, New Hampshire, North Carolina, and Vermont.

tions. But, on the other hand, if the statute of Edward III is controlling, an alien is entitled to serve on a jury trying another alien. Both legal principles existed before the settlement of America. Hence, the question from the American point of view would seem to be whether or not the statute of Edward was local in nature and, therefore, not a part of that body of law brought over to this country.

Only one case has been found relating to this situation. The North Carolina Code provision (2312) does not stipulate that jurors must be citizens. The court of that state held that while alienage is not a statutory disqualification, such status was a disqualification at common law. The opinion went on to point out that the state statute had not modified the common law and therefore alienage was considered a disqualification by the North Carolina court.[10]

It is evident that this decision was premised upon the position taken in a much earlier case,[11] namely, that the statute of Edward was local in nature and hence not a part of the inherited body of law. No cases have been found on this point in the other four jurisdictions.[12] However, in these states it would be necessary for the courts to determine whether or not the statute of Edward was local in its effect before it would be possible to determine the alien's right to serve on a jury.

This discussion began as a consideration of an alien's right to a jury de medietate linguae, and at first glance it would seem to have resolved itself into a consideration of the right of an alien to serve on a jury. However, this seemingly inconsistent discussion is germane to the subject under consideration. It is necessary to determine an alien's right to serve on a jury before any conclusions can be drawn as to the alien's right to trial by a jury de medietate linguae. For if the alien may not serve on a jury, then it would be

[10] *Hinton v. Hinton.*
[11] *State v. Antonio.*
[12] Note 9 above.

impossible to impanel a jury of one half aliens in order to extend the right to a trial jury of this nature.

Forty-three states have specifically stipulated that jurors must, among other things, be citizens.[18] Therefore, as far as these states are concerned, the statement made by Mr. Justice Preston, that "it may fairly be considered, that our statutes directing specially how our juries shall be composed, and enumerating their qualifications, and especially that the lawful juror shall be a citizen of the State, have abolished the right to a jury *de medietate linguae,* if it ever existed in Louisiana,"[14] would be true in all these states. The remaining five states do not specifically include citizenship among the qualifications required for jurors. The one case that has been found in this connection considered the statute of Edward local in nature, and by giving this interpretation to its effect the older provision of the common law was made controlling. The result of this position is that the alien, at least so far as North Carolina is concerned, does not have the right to a jury de medietate linguae because of the impossibility legally of having any alien jurors.

The interpretation of the common law, applicable in this country as made by the North Carolina court, seems to be the more sound of the two possible interpretations. When the statute of Edward was enacted, English public policy had for one of its purposes the attracting of aliens to England, and the statute was one of the inducements offered. The same may or may not have been true in the early history of the United States. Whether it was or not is no longer of any importance. The present policy of the United States is to limit the coming of aliens to this country.

In the second place, there are certain practical considerations which would seem to substantiate the belief that the statute of Edward was local in nature. Between the time of the enactment of the statute and American independence

---

[18] See below, Appendix D.   [14] *State v. Fuentes.*

aliens followed the practice of living in compact groups in England, and it was an easy matter for the courts to find a sufficient number of aliens whenever the occasion for their services arose. In the United States this concentration of alien population is not and has never been carried to the degree that prevailed in England. It is highly improbable that in every county in the five states a jury composed of one half aliens speaking the same language as the accused alien could be found. The officer in charge of impaneling the jury could not go hunting about the state for the requisite number of aliens because that would violate the laws requiring a jury of persons from the county or circuit in which the court was sitting. And on the other hand, a jury de medietate linguae could not be granted to those alien defendants who were of the nationality which had a sufficient number of representatives in the county to make up the jury while it was denied other aliens not having enough of their fellow nationals living in the court's jurisdiction. For a state to give such a jury to one type of alien because it was possible to collect a jury and to deny it to another because it was impossible, would cause the state no end of trouble arising out of the Fourteenth Amendment to the United States Constitution, not to mention its own constitution and laws. In no state has the alien a right to a jury de medietate linguae: in forty-three states the citizenship requirement makes such a jury impossible, and in the remaining five the North Carolina court's interpretation of the common law—valid for American purposes—is weighty, if not adequate, reason for not granting such a jury in these five states. Some states have specifically denied aliens the right to such a jury.[15]

One state code provides for a jury de medietate linguae. The Kentucky Code (2254) provides that the courts, in their

[15] For example, see codes of Alabama, 8615; Michigan, 1929; Pennsylvania, 12949; Illinois, 38:740; and Maryland, 51:18.

discretion, may grant such a jury to an alien. Counsel for an alien defendant demanded such a jury for his client as of right. Mr. Justice Carroll, in writing the opinion, took occasion to express in very unequivocal terms his dissatisfaction with such a provision in an American code of laws. This section, he said, "stands now and has always stood apart from all other sections of the statutes relating to the selection of juries, and has never had any orderly connection with the elaborate system of laws treating of this subject, that from time to time have been enacted. Not only so, but this privilege allowed aliens is, and has always been, contrary to the spirit of American institutions and the public policy of this country." After having expressed his feelings in the matter along these lines, the judge then addressed himself to the question of the *right* belonging to the alien under Kentucky law.

The statute provides that such a jury "may be directed by court"—not that it shall be—and when we consider that there is every reason why such a jury should not be allowed, and no apparent reason exists why it should, we think that the disposition of the matter should be left to the discretion of the trial court, subject to review of this court in any case in which it is made clearly to appear that the discretion has been abused.[16]

Therefore, in the one state which provides for such a jury it is not the alien's right, but a matter for the court's discretion. Furthermore, it should be noticed that this provision creates an anomalous situation in that the section of the Kentucky Code immediately preceding this one specifically provides that jurors in Kentucky must be citizens. No case has been found which clarifies this contradiction.

Whether an alien may have a jury de medietate linguae in the United States courts depends upon the law of the state in which the court is sitting. The federal court can-

[16] *Wendling v. Commonwealth* (1911), 137 S. W. (Ky.) 205.

not impanel such a jury if it is not within the power of the state court so to do.[17]

Having considered the alien's right to serve on a jury, attention is now to be turned to a consideration of the alien's right to trial by jury.[18] The right to trial by jury in the United States courts is protected by the Sixth and Seventh Amendments to the United States Constitution. The so-called federal bill of rights embraced in the first ten amendments is restrictive only of action by the national government and does not apply to state governments.[19] The Sixth Amendment assures a jury trial in criminal prosecutions. This protection extends not only to citizens, but also to aliens accused of crime.[20] The Seventh Amendment extends and assures a jury trial in civil cases, that is to say, "in Suits at common law, where the value in controversy shall exceed twenty dollars."[21]

It is difficult to see how an alien would not be entitled to national treatment in the matter of jury trial in the federal courts. It is beyond the scope of this project to enter into all the ramifications of the problem of jury trial in this country. It is realized that the elusive "due process" clause of the Fifth Amendment does not require a jury trial in every conceivable and possible case that may come up in the courts.[22] However, the Sixth and Seventh Amendments, in that they apply to "persons," do extend to aliens every-

[17] *Kentucky v. Wendling* (1910), 182 Fed. 140.
[18] It is beyond the scope of this study to consider the matter of jury trial in exclusion and deportation cases. This study is concerned only with the rights of aliens who are legally in the country and who continue to be legally entitled to remain. For an excellent treatment of deportation problems see W. C. Van Vleck, *The Administrative Control of Aliens.*
[19] *Barron v. Baltimore* (1833), 7 Pet. 243.
[20] *Colyer v. Skeffington* (1920), 265 Fed. 17.
[21] Such trial relates only to United States courts. *Pearson v. Yewdall* (1877), 95 U. S. 294. It is not a limitation on the state courts. *Slocum v. New York Life Insurance Co.* (1913), 228 U. S. 364; *Railroad Co. v. Bombolis* (1916), 241 U. S. 211.
[22] F. Frankfurter and T. G. Corcoran, "Petty Federal Offenses and the Constitutional Guaranty of Trial by Jury," 39 *Harvard Law Rev.* 917-982.

thing that is embraced in the amendments for the protection of citizens.

The United States Constitution does not impose upon the state governments the obligation of providing for a jury trial either in criminal or civil cases. The existence of such a right in state courts is dependent upon state constitutions and laws. It has been contended that the "due process" clause of the Fourteenth Amendment requires that states shall provide for a jury trial. This contention is not accepted by the United States Supreme Court.[23]

However, the Fourteenth Amendment protects aliens as well as citizens, and the "equal protection of the laws" clause therein is a "pledge of the protection of equal laws."[24] Therefore, it is believed that the Fourteenth Amendment, although not prohibiting the abolition of jury trial in state courts, does protect the alien against unequal treatment in this matter and thereby assures him national treatment in state courts. To summarize the alien's right to a jury trial in this country, the following quotation may be made from an opinion handed down in the Missouri state court: "An alien committing a crime in violation of our laws is meted out the same measure of justice and *according to the same forms of procedure* that is accorded to our own citizens, and with this he must be satisfied."[25]

The Fourteenth Amendment prohibits state governments from enacting any legislation which would attempt to try aliens not "according to the same forms of procedure" which are extended to citizens.

[23] *Walker v. Sauvinet* (1875), 92 U. S. 90.
[24] *Yick Wo v. Hopkins* (1886), 118 U. S. 356.
[25] *State v. Neighbaker* (1904), 184 Mo. 211. Italics mine.

VII

SUMMARY AND CONCLUSION

THERE HAS BEEN an expansion of the rights of aliens and methods of protecting these rights against infringement. In the opening chapter an examination was made of the rights and privileges which aliens enjoy by virtue of customary international law. In the second chapter was discussed the extent to which this list of rights and privileges has been expanded by the United States government and its cosignatories through treaty arrangements. That the number of rights and the extent of enjoyment thereof have been expanded is made evident by the most casual examination of the customary law and treaties.

This was preliminary to the main purpose of the study, which is an inquiry into the extent to which aliens are accorded national treatment by virtue of American municipal law. So far as aliens in the United States are concerned, they have by virtue of Amercan constitutional and statutory law a greater latitude of enjoyment and protection than either customary or conventional international law demands. This is made possible by the fact that throughout American municipal law, both national and state, the term "persons" is widely used when that law relates to personal rights or, to express it more technically, civil rights. Courts have been remarkably hesitant in giving an interpretation which would tend to limit the meaning of "persons."

Equality, as between aliens and citizens, in the enjoyment of many rights is so well established as to make it seem unnecessary and unjustifiable to consider these rights in this study. On the other hand, there are rights and privileges the equal enjoyment of which has given rise to litigation. It is with these that this inquiry is concerned. The principles and arguments brought forth to deny equality, and the attitude of the courts and legislatures toward such objections have been discussed. The result of such an investigation leads to the conclusion that in nearly all civil rights *resident* aliens enjoy a treatment which is equal to that of American nationals. Moreover, no provision of either customary or conventional international law has been found which extends equal treatment to any personal civil rights which the alien, resident in the United States, does not enjoy by virtue of American municipal law. In other words, international law as it stands today does not elaborate or extend the personal rights which resident aliens enjoy beyond the limits prescribed by American municipal law. What is accomplished is the placing of a somewhat less extensive category of personal rights under the protection of international law. That is to say, those personal rights which exist by virtue of international law as well as municipal law may not be rescinded merely by modifying municipal law. International law offers an additional source of protection rather than a source of expansion, and any municipal interference with the rights would create an international obligation and subject the United States to liability for such violation.

International customary law prescribes a minimum standard of treatment which all members of the family of nations must accord aliens within their jurisdictions. The scope of this minimum standard is exceedingly controversial. There seems to be unanimity among publicists and tribunals that aliens are entitled to "life, liberty and property" while resident outside their own country. The controversy among publicists centers around the problem of whether or not customary international law prescribes a minimum standard of treatment which goes beyond "life, liberty and property." Regardless of any opinion motivated by humanitarian considerations which would tend to induce agreement with publicists of more liberal proclivities, the fact remains that any minimum standard which goes beyond "life, liberty and property" is questionable law. To espouse this extended minimum standard of treatment would place the advocate on the defensive and subject him to the necessity of employing arguments of dubious validity. The most that can be accepted with any degree of certainty is that international customary law as it is today protects the "life, liberty and property" of aliens and no more. Even this is not as extensive as it might appear. For example, in connection with property customary international law does not require that states extend to aliens the right to acquire real property.

The provisions of customary international law are not national treatment provisions in the true sense. The term national treatment means the extension of a treatment to aliens which is equal to that accorded by the state to its own nationals. The provisions of international customary law do not seek to establish equality of enjoyment of the rights of "life, liberty and property." Customary law requires that aliens are to enjoy these rights or privileges not to an extent to which nationals enjoy them, but rather to an extent determined by an international standard of treatment. This, obviously, makes it possible for aliens in a given country to enjoy these privileges to a greater extent than nationals of the country.

National treatment is the result of conventional international law and municipal law. Inasmuch as there is a great body of treaty provisions extending national treatment to aliens, international conventional law must be considered as a source of national treatment. Treaty provisions of this nature are to be found with increasing frequency and scope in international commitments. The United States government has entered into a number of them. The scope, nature, and purpose of such provisions were considered in the second chapter. The earlier treaties were more restricted in that their national treatment provisions were almost exclusively confined to matters of navigation. As the number of aliens resident in this country, as well as the number of Americans resident abroad, increased, there was a concurrent expansion of national treatment provisions. This expansion was along lines not necessarily connected with navigation. There resulted a development of national treatment provisions in the direction of granting civil rights and commercial privileges generally.

The purpose of investigating the rights accorded aliens by virtue of American municipal law was to determine whether, and the extent to which, aliens in this country enjoy greater rights by virtue of American municipal law than those required by the treaty commitments to which this country is bound. All of the municipal law rights of aliens were not considered. The discussion was confined to those rights about which there was dispute and doubt. The others are so well established that they do not warrant discussion. Investigation of the rights of aliens having a controversial aspect demonstrates that the treaty provisions add very little if anything to that which foreigners have by virtue of municipal law in this country.

The evidence adduced from the investigation of this whole topic seems to justify several general conclusions. Traditionally, there has existed a distinct difference of political and civil status between aliens and nationals. States have accorded more actual rights to their nationals, as well as a greater degree of protection of those rights. In the earlier years of the history of the modern period, aliens were sometimes grossly discriminated against, if tolerated at all. One of the developments of modern political philosophy, that is, national treatment of aliens, grew out of carrying to its logical conclusion the concept of the "rights of man."

Regardless of when this doctrine had its origin, it would seem correct to say that it was for the modern world to give the concept whatever claim it may have to practical application. It is conceded that the concept falls far short of achieving what some of its proponents had hoped. However, it cannot be denied that it has profoundly influenced modern political philosophy and development.

In a world that is conscious of the existence of such a concept, that has more or less made an effort to bring about its realization, it is only logical that its corollary should be the alleviation of the onerous treatment traditionally accorded aliens. To be sure, it is doubtful if the limited acceptance of the doctrine of the "rights of man" can justifiably be considered as the explanation of the gradual diminution of discrimination against aliens that has been taking place. It is not suggested that this is the cause, or even the most important factor. It is suggested that the acceptance of this philosophy created a congenial frame of mind, so to speak, for the development which has taken place in national policy toward aliens and their rights. A more important factor, impelling governments to lessen discrimination against aliens and increasingly to extend to them treatment which is equal to that extended their own nationals, is the economic one.

One bit of evidence in support of the opinion that the economic factor is very important is furnished by the treaties entered into by the commercial nations during the last hundred years. As world commerce has increased, there has been an increase in the liberality of alien treatment which is too consistent and concurrent to be dismissed as a mere coincidence. Moreover, in a consideration of the treaties of one commercial country, the United States, the fact is demonstrated that the United States government extends national treatment in a greater degree to those countries with which it has the greater volume of foreign trade.

The economic factor, important as it is, is not a complete and adequate explanation of the American policy toward aliens. No doubt it has played a very important part, but it certainly has not been the sole cause. The national and state constitutions and laws in this country have extended protection of the more fundamental personal rights of individuals to "persons" rather than to citizens. In interpreting the constitutions and laws, the courts have consistently been of the opinion that the term "persons" was consciously and purposely used in order that all individuals, whether aliens or citizens, should be granted whatever protection is accorded by law. It is suggested that in this respect the doctrine of the "rights of man" has had its greatest influence.[1]

It might be suggested that the reason for this constitutional phenomenon in the United States is that there was need to attract immigrants for the population of a sparsely populated area. It cannot be denied that there is a measure of truth in this hypothesis, but to maintain that it is the final explanation would seem to ignore some very pertinent and inescapable facts. If the constitutions that have been adopted since the American Constitution by the various countries of the world, and more particularly those that have come into being since the World War,[2] are scrutinized, such an investigation will demonstrate the fact that by and large national constitutions have become increasingly liberal in their extension of rights and protection therefor to persons rather than merely to nationals. This is equally true of countries that are, and of those that are not, compelled by the

[1] See the draft convention formulated by the Institute of International Law, 35 *Annuaire*, pt. 2, 117.

[2] C. E. Martin and W. H. George, *Representative Modern Constitutions;* A. Headlam-Morley, *The New Democratic Constitutions of Europe;* H. L. McBain and L. Rogers, *The New Constitutions of Europe.*

forces of international trade to seek the goodwill of other countries by extending liberal treatment to aliens in order to court favor for commercial reasons. In other words, one of the reasons for a commercial country's consciously or unconsciously adopting a liberal policy is to gain the goodwill of other countries, which is always conducive to foreign trade. On the other hand, this is not as great an influence in countries which do not enjoy a great volume of foreign trade. The same liberal policy is developing in countries which may be accused of having commercial motives and in those against which such an accusation is not so easily made. Although commerce is a very important force, it is apparently not the only factor. Moreover, to contend that commercial countries, such as the United States, have been motivated exclusively by the supposed more practical reasons of commerce is an inadequate explanation. It seems to leave too much unexplained. But regardless of whether governments have adopted a more liberal attitude toward aliens for economic, philosophical, or even mystical reasons, the fact remains that this greater liberality of treatment is legally assured and is one of the characteristics of modern political control.

Recent events in the so-called dictatorial or totalitarian states would seem to invalidate this reasoning. These states, however, are exceptional. The condition of aliens in most of the states of the world is what it was before the coming of such dictatorial philosophy and organization of government. We must guard against allowing these dramatic exceptions to be considered the rule. One cannot say whether they are temporary exceptions or whether they are portents of what is to be universal. But this much is true: at the present time they are exceptions, and one can hope, and even feel reasonably assured, that they shall be exceptions of a more or less temporary nature.

The nature of the municipal law of the world taken *in*

toto has a great influence in determining the nature of international law. This is evident with respect to the treatment of aliens. As more and more governments adopted a more liberal policy toward aliens, the respective states contributed to the ultimate universal validity of the various rights which they recognized as belonging to aliens. The more universally a given right is recognized as appertaining to aliens, the more likely is there to develop the establishment of that right as one existing in international law and receiving protection therefrom. That is to say, a point is ultimately reached where a government recognizes in its municipal law that certain rights appertain to aliens. It is also cognizant of the fact that most of the other governments of the world recognize the same rights as belonging to aliens within their respective jurisdictions. On the basis of these two factors a government will protest the denial of these rights to its nationals by another government, and, by virtue of international customary law, will be able to secure recognition of the rights by the offending government.

One of the tests applied to a principle of international law to determine its validity is whether or not the principle in question is generally consented to and considered by the members of the family of nations as binding upon themselves. Most publicists subscribe to this "consent" theory of international law. It is their opinion that a state, generally speaking, is bound only by those rules to which it has expressly or tacitly consented. This is the normal interpretation of the position of international law.[3]

On the other hand, there is a minority of publicists who maintain that international law is a part of the whole legal system and inseparable from municipal law. Typical proponents of the "monist" theory are Lauterpacht[4] and the

---

[3] For example, J. L. Brierly, *The Law of Nations;* L. Oppenheim, *International Law.*

[4] *Private Law Sources and Analogies of International Law,* and *The Function of Law in the International Community.*

"Vienna School." Lauterpacht is of the opinion that international law is founded in municipal law, and he establishes its unity with municipal law through the process of analogy. The "Vienna School" use the reverse technique. They work from international law to municipal law, placing the latter in an inferior position.[5]

Any attempt to determine which of these two conflicting theories explains the proper nature of international law is not germane to this discussion. To attempt an explanation of how certain municipal law principles have influenced the establishment of customary international law is not to say that municipal law grows into international law. What has happened is that certain municipal law principles have been adopted by international law in order to give them a more extensive, an international, protection. Governments generally have circumscribed their freedom in treatment of aliens by their own municipal law. This indicates a wide acceptance of the municipal law principle that certain rights appertain to the individual whether he is alien or citizen. The general acceptance of this principle is indicative of the existence in the political thinking of the world of that which makes possible the acceptance of the principle as a rule of international law. It is because of the universality of this *attitude* that customary international law rules for the protection of alien rights have come into existence, and, by virtue of these rules, a state which refuses to extend such rights to aliens may be called upon as of right to make reparation.

Customary international law naturally protects the least number of rights which aliens enjoy. Many nations have found it expedient, if not necessary, to elaborate and extend

---

[5] For an excellent statement of the case for the "Vienna School" see J. L. Kunz, "The 'Vienna School' and International Law," 11 *N. Y. Univ. Law Quar. Rev.* 370-421. See also H. Kelsen, *Das Problem der Souveränität und die Theorie des Völkerrechts,* and A. Verdross, *Die Einheit des rechtlichen Weltbildes.*

rights through treaty arrangements. The treaty method not only offers an opportunity for two or more states to extend the rights to be enjoyed by their nationals while in the jurisdiction of the other contracting parties, but has the further advantage of recommitting the signatories to the principles (fewer in number) that exist in customary law. In short, it removes doubt as to the existence of the principles, at least as far as the relationships of the contracting parties are concerned. For this reason, many treaties have been entered into which contain national treatment provisions. As this conventional expansion of alien rights becomes more and more universal, the added rights come nearer and nearer to being included in the customary law. Or, as one writer has expressed it:

Since they are binding upon the parties to them, treaties may be regarded as evidence of what the states, bound by their terms, accept at the time as law. When the same terms are generally accepted among nations, treaties become a valuable evidence as to practice and are regarded as proper sources of international law, or principles may be so well established by successive treaties as to need no further treaty specification.[6]

Herein lies, for international law and its development, the significance of much of the practice of assuring national treatment to aliens in the United States.

[6] G. G. Wilson, *International Law*, p. 40. From *International Law*, copyright 1935, by permission of the author, George Grafton Wilson, and the publisher, Silver, Burdett and Company.

APPENDICES

APPENDIX A

CITATIONS OF NATIONAL TREATMENT PROVISIONS IN
AMERICAN TREATIES*

1. RIGHT TO ENTER, TRAVEL, SOJOURN

Name of State	Date	Article	U. S. Statute
Austria	1829	I	8: 399
*Austria	1928	I	47:1877
*Bolivia	1858	III	12:1004
Congo	1891	I	27: 927
Corea	1882	VI	23: 720
Dominican Republic	1867	III	15: 475
*Esthonia	1925	I & XV	44:2379, 2384
*Germany	1923	I & XVI	44:2133, 2146
Great Britain	1794	XIV	8: 124
*Great Britain	1871	XXVII	17: 872
Greece	1837	I	8: 498
Hanover	1846	X	9: 864
Haiti	1864	VI	13: 713
*Honduras	1927	I & XV	45:2618, 2629
*Hungary	1925	I & XIII	44:2441,2453
*Italy	1871	I & II	17: 845, 846
Japan	1894	I	29: 848
Japan	1911	I	37:1504
*Latvia	1928	I	45:2643
Mecklenburg-Schwerin	1847	X	9: 918
Nicaragua	1867	IX	15: 555
*Norway	1928	I & XV	47:2136, 2146
Peru	1851	II	10: 927
Peru	1870	II	18: 699
*Poland	1931	I	48:1507
Portugal	1840	I	8: 560
Prussia	1828	I	8: 378
Russia	1832	I	8: 444
Salvador	1870	XXXIX	18: 740
*Salvador	1926	I & XIV	46:2818, 2827
*Serbia	1881	I	22: 963

* Treaties marked (*) still in force.

*Siam	1920	I	42:1928
*Spain	1902	II	33:2106
*Swiss Confederation	1850	I	11: 587
*Tonga	1886	III	25:1441
Venezuela	1836	III	8: 466
Venezuela	1850	III	12:1144

2. RIGHT TO ENGAGE IN WORK

Austria	1829	I	8: 399
*Austria	1928	I	47:1877
Belgium	1845	I	8: 606
Belgium	1858	I	12:1043
*Belgium	1875	I	19: 628
*Bolivia	1858	III	12:1004
*Brazil	1828	III	8: 390
Central America	1825	III	8: 322
Congo	1891	I	27: 927
*Denmark	1826	II	8: 340
Dominican Republic	1867	III	15: 475
Ecuador	1839	III	8: 534
*Esthonia	1925	I	44:2379
*Germany	1923	I	44:2133
Great Britain	1794	XIV	8: 124
Guatemala	1849	III	10: 874
Haiti	1864	VI	13: 713
*Honduras	1927	I	45:2618
*Hungary	1925	I	44:2441
*Italy	1871	II	17: 846
Japan	1894	II	29: 849
Japan	1911	I	37:1504
*Latvia	1928	I	45:2643
*New Granada	1846	III	9: 882
*Norway	1928	I	47:2136
*Paraguay	1859	IX	12:1095
Peru	1851	II	10: 927
Peru	1870	II	18: 699
Peru	1887	II	25:1445
*Poland	1931	I	48:1507
Portugal	1840	I	8: 560
Russia	1832	I	8: 444
Salvador	1850	III	10: 891
Salvador	1870	III	18: 726
*Salvador	1926	I	46:2818
*Serbia	1881	I	22: 963
*Siam	1920	I	42:1928
*Spain	1902	II	33:2106
*Swiss Confederation	1850	I	11: 587
Two Sicilies	1855	VI	11: 643
Venezuela	1836	III	8: 466
Venezuela	1860	III	12:1144

3. Right to Acquire Real and Personal Property

*Argentina	1853	IX	10:1009
*Austria	1928	I	47:1877
*Bolivia	1858	III	12:1004
Corea	1882	VI	23: 720
Dominican Republic	1867	III	15: 475
*Esthonia	1925	I	44:2379
*Germany	1923	I	44:2133
Great Britain	1794	XIV	8: 124
Greece	1837	I	8: 498
Haiti	1864	VI	13: 713
Hanover	1846	X	9: 864
Hawaii	1849	VIII	9: 979
*Honduras	1927	I	45:2618
*Hungary	1925	I	44:2441
*Italy	1871	II	17: 846
Japan	1894	II	29: 849
Japan	1911	I	37:1504
Latvia	1928	I	45:2643
Mecklenburg-Schwerin	1847	X	9: 918
Peru	1870	II	18: 699
Peru	1887	II	25:1445
*Poland	1931	I	48:1507
Salvador	1850	III	10: 891
Salvador	1870	III	18: 726
*Salvador	1926	I	46:2818
*Serbia	1881	II	22: 964
*Siam	1920	I	42:1928
*Swiss Confederation	1850	I	11: 587
*Tonga	1886	III	25:1441
Two Sicilies	1845	VI	9: 836
Two Sicilies	1855	VI	11: 643
Venezuela	1860	III	12:1144

4. Protection Against Illegal Search and Seizure

*Austria	1928	III	47:1879
*Bolivia	1858	III	12:1004
Congo	1891	III	27: 928
*Esthonia	1925	III	44:2380
*Germany	1923	III	44:2134
Haiti	1864	VII	13: 714
Hawaii	1849	VIII	9: 979
*Honduras	1927	III	45:2620
*Hungary	1925	III	44:2443
Japan	1894	III	29: 849
Japan	1911	II	37:1505
*Latvia	1928	III	45:2643
*Norway	1928	III	47:2137
Peru	1851	II	10: 927
Peru	1870	II	18: 699
Peru	1887	II	25:1445

*Poland	....	1931	III	48:1507
*Salvador	....	1926	III	46:2819
*Serbia	....	1881	IV	22: 965
*Siam	....	1920	II	42:1929
*Spain	....	1902	VI	33:2108
Two Sicilies	....	1845	VI	9: 837
Two Sicilies	....	1855	V	11: 643

5. PROTECTION OF PERSONS AND PROPERTY

*Argentina	....	1853	VIII, IX, X & XII	10:1008-1010
*Austria	....	1928	I & II	47:1877, 1878
Belgium	....	1845	I	8: 606
Belgium	....	1858	I	12:1043
*Belgium	....	1875	I	19: 628
*Bolivia	....	1858	III & XIII	12:1004, 1010
*Brazil	....	1828	XII	8: 392
Central America	....	1825	XII	8: 326
Chile	....	1832	X	8: 436
Colombia	....	1824	X	8: 310
Congo	....	1891	I	27: 927
*Costa Rica	....	1851	VII, VIII, IX & XI	10: 920-922
Dominican Republic	......	1867	II	15: 474
Ecuador	....	1839	XIII	8: 538
*Esthonia	....	1925	I & II	44:2379, 2380
*Germany	....	1923	I & II	44:2133, 2134
Great Britain	....	1794	XIV	8: 124
Guatemala	....	1849	XII	10: 878
Haiti	....	1864	V	13: 713
Hanseatic Republics	......	1827	VIII	8: 370
Hawaii	....	1849	VIII	9: 979
Honduras	....	1864	VII, VIII, IX & XI	13: 703-706
*Honduras	....	1927	I & II	45:2618, 2620
*Hungary	....	1925	I & II	44:2441, 2443
*Italy	....	1871	III	17: 846
*Italy	....	1913	I	38:1670
Japan	....	1894	I	29: 848
Japan	....	1911	I	37:1504
*Latvia	....	1928	I & II	45:2643
Mexico	....	1831	IX & XIV	8: 414, 416
*New Granada	....	1846	XIII	9: 886
Nicaragua	....	1867	VII & IX	15: 553, 555
*Norway	....	1928	I & II	47:2136, 2137
Orange Free State	....	1871	II	18: 749
*Paraguay	....	1859	IX & X	12:1095
Peru-Bolivia	....	1836	IX	8: 489
Peru	....	1851	XIX	10: 934
Peru	....	1870	II & XVI	18: 699, 705
Peru	....	1887	II & XV	25:1445, 1451
*Poland	....	1931	I & II	48:1507
Portugal	....	1840	I	8: 560
Prussia	....	1828	I	8: 378

Salvador	1850	XIII	10: 893
Salvador	1870	XIII & XXIX	18: 730, 739
*Salvador	1926	I & II	46:2818, 2819
Sardinia	1838	I	8: 512
*Serbia	1881	I & IV	22: 963, 964
*Siam	1920	I	42:1928
*Spain	1902	II	33:2106
*Swiss Confederation	1850	II	11: 589
*Tonga	1886	IX	25:1442
Two Sicilies	1845	VI	9: 837
Two Sicilies	1855	I, II & V	11: 640, 643
Venezuela	1836	XIII	8: 472
Venezuela	1860	II	12:1144
*Conv. on Industrial Property	1925	II	47:1797
*Conv. on Status of Aliens..	1928	III	46:2754

6. PROTECTION OF TRADE-MARKS AND PATENTS

*Denmark	1892	I	27: 963
*Guatemala	1906	I	35:1878
*Hungary	1912	I	37:1632
*Japan	1905	I	34:2890
Japan	1911	XV	37:1508
*Luxemburg	1904	I	34:2868
*Rumania	1906	I	34:2901
*Siam	1920	XII	42:1932
Conv. on Industrial Property	1883	II	25:1375
*Conv. on Industrial Property	1911	II	38:1660
*Pan-American Convention..	1910	III	38:1787
*Pan-American Convention..	1910	II	38:1813
*Pan-American Convention..	1929	I	46:2912

7. INTERNAL CHARGES AND TAXES

*Austria	1928	I	47:1877
Belgium	1845	I	8: 606
Belgium	1858	I	12:1043
*Belgium	1875	I	19: 628
*Bolivia	1858	III	12:1004
Congo	1891	I	27: 927
Dominican Republic	1867	II	15: 474
Ecuador	1839	VII	8: 536
*Esthonia	1925	I	44:2379
*Germany	1923	I	44:2133
Haiti	1864	V	13: 713
Honduras	1864	IX	13: 704
*Honduras	1927	I	45:2618
*Hungary	1925	I	44:2441
Japan	1894	I	29: 848
Japan	1911	I	37:1504
*Latvia	1928	I	45:2643
Nicaragua	1867	IX	15: 555
*Norway	1928	I	47:2136

Orange Free State	1871	I & II	18: 749, 750
*Paraguay	1859	XI	12:1096
Peru	1851	II	10: 927
Peru	1870	II	18: 699
Peru	1887	II	25:1445
*Poland	1931	I	48:1507
Salvador	1870	XXIX	18: 739
*Salvador	1926	I	46:2818
*Serbia	1881	I	22: 963
*Siam	1920	I	42:1928
*Spain	1902	II	33:2106
*Swiss Confederation	1850	I & II	11: 587, 589
*Tonga	1886	IX	25:1442
Two Sicilies	1855	V	11: 640

8. Access to Courts; Punishments

*Argentina	1853	VIII & IX	10:1008, 1009
*Austria	1928	I	47:1877
*Bolivia	1858	XIII	12:1010
*Brazil	1828	XII	8: 392
Central America	1825	XII	8: 326
Chile	1832	X	8: 436
Colombia	1824	X	8: 310
Congo	1891	III	27: 928
*Costa Rica	1851	VII & VIII	10: 920, 921
Dominican Republic	1867	III	15: 475
Ecuador	1839	XIII	8: 538
*Esthonia	1925		44:2379
*Germany	1923	I	44:2133
Guatemala	1849	XII	10: 878
Haiti	1864	VI	13: 713
Hanover	1840	I	8: 552
Hanover	1846	X	9: 865
Hanseatic Republics	1827	VIII	8: 370
Honduras	1864	VII & VIII	13: 703
*Honduras	1927	I	45:2618
*Hungary	1925	I	44:2441
*Italy	1871	XXIII	17: 856
Japan	1894	I	29: 848
Mecklenburg-Schwerin	1847	X	9: 918
Mexico	1831	XIV	8: 416
Netherlands	1782	VII	8: 36
*New Granada	1846	XIII	9: 886
Nicaragua	1867	VII	15: 553
*Norway	1928	I	47:2136
*Paraguay	1859	IX & X	12:1095
Peru-Bolivia	1836	IX	8: 489
Peru	1851	XIX	10: 934
Peru	1870	XVI	18: 705
Peru	1887	XV	25:1451
Salvador	1850	XIII	10: 893

Salvador	1870	XIII	18: 730
*Salvador	1926	I	46:2818
*Serbia	1881	IV	22: 965
*Siam	1920	IV	42:1929
Spain	1795	XX	8: 150
*Spain	1898	XI	30:2108
*Swiss Confederation	1850	I	11: 587
Two Sicilies	1855	VII	11: 644
Venezuela	1836	XIII	8: 472
Venezuela	1860	III	12:1144

9. Inheritance and Transmission of Property

*Argentina	1853	IX	10:1009
Austria	1829	XI	8: 401
Austria	1848	I & II	9: 944, 945
*Austria	1928	IV	47:1879
Bavaria	1845	II & III	9: 827
*Bolivia	1858	XII	12:1010
*Brazil	1828	XI	8: 392
Brunswick	1854	I & II	11: 601, 602
Central America	1825	XI	8: 326
Chile	1832	IX	8: 435
Colombia	1824	IX	8: 308
*Costa Rica	1851	VIII	10: 921
Dominican Republic	1867	V	15: 476
Ecuador	1839	XII	8: 538
*Esthonia	1925	IV	44:2380
France	1778	XI	8: 18
France	1800	VII	8: 182
France	1853	VII	10: 996
*Germany	1923	IV	47:2135
Great Britain	1794	IX	8: 122
*Great Britain	1899	I & II	31:1939
Guatemala	1849	XI	10: 878
*Guatemala	1901	I & II	32:1945
Haiti	1864	IX	13: 714
Hanover	1840	VII	8: 556
Hanover	1846	X	9: 865
Hanseatic Republics	1827	VII	8: 370
Hawaii	1849	VIII	9: 979
Hesse-Cassel	1844	II & III	9: 818, 819
Honduras	1864	VIII	13: 703
*Honduras	1927	IV	45:2620
*Hungary	1925	IV	44:2443
*Italy	1871	XXII	17: 856
Japan	1894	I	29: 848
*Latvia	1928	IV	45:2643
Mecklenburg-Schwerin	1847	X	9: 918
Mexico	1831	XIII	8: 414
Nassau	1846	II & III	9: 850
Netherlands	1782	VI	8: 36

*New Granada	1846	XII	9: 886
Nicaragua	1867	VIII	16: 553
*Norway	1928	IV	47:2138
Orange Free State	1871	III	18: 750
*Paraguay	1859	X	12:1095
Peru-Bolivia	1836	VIII	8: 489
Peru	1851	XV	10: 932
Peru	1870	XII	18: 703
Peru	1887	XI	25:1449
*Poland	1931	IV	48:1507
Portugal	1840	XII	8: 566
Prussia	1785	X	8: 88
Prussia	1799	X	8: 166
Prussia	1828	XIV	8: 384
Russia	1832	X	8: 448
Salvador	1850	XII	10: 893
Salvador	1870	XII & XXVIII	18: 730, 738
*Salvador	1926	IV	46:2820
Sardinia	1838	XVIII	8: 520
Saxony	1845	II & III	8: 830, 831
*Serbia	1881	II	22: 964
Spain	1795	XI	8: 144
*Spain	1902	III	33:2107
Sweden	1783	VI	8: 64
*Sweden	1910	XIV	37:1488
Swiss Confederation	1847	I & II	9: 902, 903
*Swiss Confederation	1850	V	11: 590
Two Sicilies	1845	VI	9: 836
Two Sicilies	1855	VI	11: 643
Venezuela	1836	XII	8: 470
Venezuela	1860	V	12:1146
Württemberg	1844	II & III	8: 588

10. LIBERTY OF CONSCIENCE AND FREEDOM OF WORSHIP

*Argentina	1853	XIII	10:1011
*Austria	1928	I & V	47:1877, 1880
*Bolivia	1858	XIV	12:1011
*Brazil	1828	XIII	8: 393
Central America	1825	XIII	8: 328
Chile	1832	XI	8: 436
*China	1868	IV	16: 740
Colombia	1824	XI	8: 310
Congo	1891	IV	27: 928
*Costa Rica	1851	XII	10: 923
Dominican Republic	1867	IV	15: 475
Ecuador	1839	XIV	8: 540
*Esthonia	1925	I & V	44:2379, 2380
*Germany	1923	I & V	44:2133, 2136
Guatemala	1849	XIII	10: 878
Haiti	1864	VIII	13: 714
Hawaii	1849	XI	9: 981

*Honduras	1927	I & V	45:2618, 2621
*Hungary	1925	I & V	44:2441, 2444
Japan	1894	I	29: 848
*Latvia	1928	I	45:2643
Mexico	1831	XV	8: 416
Netherlands	1782	IV	8: 34
*New Granada	1846	XIV	9: 887
Nicaragua	1867	XII	15: 557
*Norway	1928	I & V	47:2136, 2139
*Paraguay	1859	XIV	12:1098
Peru-Bolivia	1836	X	8: 490
Peru	1851	XX	10: 935
Peru	1870	XVII	18: 705
Peru	1887	XVI	25:1451
*Poland	1931	I	48:1507
Prussia	1785	XI	8: 90
Prussia	1799	XI	8: 166
Salvador	1850	XIV	10: 893
Salvador	1870	XIV	18: 731
*Salvador	1926	I & V	46:2818, 2821
*Siam	1920	I	42:1928
*Spain	1902	IV	33:2108
Sweden	1783	V	8: 62
*Tonga	1886	XIII	25:1443
Venezuela	1836	XIV	8: 472
Venezuela	1860	IV	12:1145

II. EQUAL TREATMENT IN MATTER OF CARRYING GOODS

*Argentina	1853	VI & IX	10:1007, 1009
Austria	1829	III & VI	8: 399, 400
*Austria	1928	VII & VIII	47:1883
Belgium	1845	VII, IX & X	8: 608, 610
Belgium	1858	VI, VII & VIII	12:1045
*Belgium	1875	V, VI & VII	19: 630
*Bolivia	1858	IV	12:1006
*Brazil	1828	IV	8: 391
Central America	1825	IV	8: 324
*China	1880	III	22: 829
*Costa Rica	1851	VI	10: 919
*Denmark	1826	III	8: 340
Dominican Republic	1867	VI	15: 477
Ecuador	1839	IV	8: 534
*Esthonia	1925	VII & VIII	44:2382
*Germany	1923	VII & VIII	44:2138, 2139
Great Britain	1794	III	8: 118
*Great Britain	1815	II	8: 229
Greece	1837	III, IV & IX	8: 500, 502
Hanover	1840	II	8: 554
Hanover	1846	I	9: 857
Hanseatic Republics	1827	I	8: 366
Hawaii	1849	III	9: 977

Honduras	1864	VI & VIII	13: 702, 703
*Honduras	1927	VI, VII & VIII	45:2622, 2625
*Hungary	1925	VII & VIII	44:2446, 2447
*Italy	1871	V	17: 847
Japan	1894	VI & VII	29: 850
Japan	1911	VI & VIII	37:1506
*Latvia	1928	VII & IX	45:2644
Mecklenburg-Schwerin	1847	I	9: 911
Mexico	1831	VI	8: 412
Netherlands	1839	I	8: 524
*Netherlands	1852	I	10: 982
*New Granada	1846	IV	9: 882
Nicaragua	1867	VI	15: 552
*Norway	1928	VII & VIII	47:2140,2143
*Paraguay	1859	VI, VIII & X	12:1094,1095
Peru	1851	V & VII	10: 928, 929
Peru	1870	V & VII	18: 700, 701
Peru	1887	IV & VI	25:1446, 1447
*Poland	1931	VI & VII	48:1509
Portugal	1840	IV, V & VI	8: 562
Prussia	1828	III & VI	8: 378, 380
Russia	1832	III & V	8: 446
Salvador	1850	IV	10: 892
Salvador	1870	IV	18: 726
*Salvador	1926	VII & VIII	46:2821, 2824
Sardinia	1838	III & V	8: 514
*Spain	1902	VIII	33:2109
Sweden-Norway	1827	III, IV & X	8: 348, 350
Turkey	1862	VII & VIII	12:1215
*Turkey	1929	III	46:2744
Two Sicilies	1845	II	9: 834
Two Sicilies	1855	X	11: 646
Venezuela	1836	IV	8: 468
Venezuela	1860	VI	12:1146

12. LOAD AND UNLOAD PARTS OF CARGO AT DIFFERENT PORTS

*Bolivia	1858	III	12:1004
Dominican Republic	1867	VII	15: 477
*Esthonia	1925	XI	44:2383
*Germany	1923	XI	44:2140
Greece	1837	XI	8: 502
*Honduras	1927	XI	45:2626
*Latvia	1928	XII	45:2645
*Norway	1928	XI	47:2144
Peru	1851	IX	10: 930
Peru	1887	VII	25:1447
*Poland	1931	X	48:1509
*Salvador	1926	XI	46:2825
*Spain	1902	IX	33:2110
Two Sicilies	1855	XIII	11: 647
Venezuela	1860	VII	12:1147

13. Charges upon Ships as Such

*Argentina	1853	V	10:1007
Austria	1829	II	8: 399
Belgium	1845	II, III & V	8: 606, 608
Belgium	1858	II, III & IV	12:1044, 1045
*Belgium	1875	II	19: 629
*Costa Rica	1851	V	10: 919
*Esthonia	1925	IX	44:2382
*Germany	1923	IX	44:2139
Greece	1837	II & VII	8: 498, 500
Hawaii	1849	IV	9: 978
Honduras	1864	V	13: 702
*Honduras	1927	IX	45:2625
Japan	1894	VIII	29: 850
Japan	1911	XI	37:1507
*Latvia	1928	X	45:2644
*Liberia	1862	III	12:1245
Madagascar	1881	IV	22: 955
Mexico	1831	V	8: 412
Netherlands	1839	II	8: 524
*Netherlands	1852	III	10: 983
Nicaragua	1867	V	15: 551
*Norway	1928	IX	47:2143
*Paraguay	1859	V	12:1093
Peru	1851	IV	10: 928
Peru	1870	IV	18: 700
Peru	1887	III	25:1446
*Poland	1931	VIII	48:1509
Portugal	1840	II	8: 560
Prussia	1828	II	8: 378
Russia	1832	II	8: 444
Salvador	1850	VI	10: 892
Salvador	1870	VI	18: 728
*Salvador	1926	IX	46:2824
Sardinia	1838	II	8: 512
*Spain	1898	XV	30:1761
*Spain	1902	VII	33:2109
Sweden	1816	II	8: 234
Sweden-Norway	1827	II	8: 346
Turkey	1862	IX	12:1215
Two Sicilies	1845	III	9: 834
Two Sicilies	1855	VIII	11: 645

14. Prohibition of Discrimination in Governmental Purchases of Goods Imported in Ships of Either Party

Austria	1829	VIII	8: 400
Greece	1837	VI	8: 500
Hanover	1840	V	8: 554
Hanover	1846	III	9: 859
Hanseatic Republics	1827	III	8: 368
Mecklenburg-Schwerin	1847	III	9: 912
Prussia	1828	VIII	8: 382

Sardinia	1838	VIII	8: 514
Two Sicilies	1845	V	9: 835
Two Sicilies	1855	XI	11: 646

15. SHIPWRECK

Belgium	1845	XVI	8: 610
Belgium	1858	XIV	12:1047
*Belgium	1875	XIII	19: 632
*Brazil	1828	X	8: 392
Central America	1825	X	8: 326
Chile	1832	VIII	8: 435
Colombia	1824	VIII	8: 308
Dominican Republic	1867	XI	15: 479
Ecuador	1839	XI	8: 538
*Esthonia	1925	XXVII	44:2389
*Germany	1923	XXVIII	44:2156
Guatemala	1849	X	10: 877
Haiti	1864	XVI	13: 717
Hanover	1840	VIII	8: 558
Hanover	1846	IV	9: 859
Hawaii	1849	XII	9: 981
*Honduras	1927	XXVII	45:2637
*Italy	1871	IX	17: 849
Japan	1894	XI	29: 852
*Latvia	1928	XXVIII	45:2646
Mecklenburg-Schwerin	1847	IV	9: 912
Mexico	1831	XII	8: 414
Netherlands	1782	XVI	8: 42
Netherlands	1839	V	8: 526
*New Granada	1846	XI	9: 886
*Norway	1928	XXVII	47:2157
Peru-Bolivia	1836	VII	8: 489
Peru	1851	XVI	10: 933
Peru	1870	XIII	18: 703
Peru	1887	XII	25:1449
*Poland	1931	XXVII	48:1511
Prussia	1785	IX	8: 88
Prussia	1799	IX	8: 166
Salvador	1850	XI	10: 893
Salvador	1870	XI	18: 729
*Salvador	1926	XXVI	46:2836
Sardinia	1838	XI	8: 516
*Siam	1920	X	42:1931
Spain	1795	X	8: 142
*Spain	1902	X	33:2110
Sweden	1816	X	8: 238
Sweden-Norway	1827	XV	8: 354
*Swiss Confederation	1850	XII	11: 593
Two Sicilies	1845	IX	9: 839
Two Sicilies	1855	XVI & XVII	11: 648, 649
Venezuela	1836	XI	8: 470
Venezuela	1860	XI	12:1149

APPENDIX B[1]

TABLE 1

STATES PERMITTING ALL ALIENS, WITHOUT DISTINCTION, TO TAKE
REAL PROPERTY BY PURCHASE

State	Citation	Remarks
Alabama	6071	
Colorado	130	
Delaware	Rev. Stat. 3194	
Georgia	79-303	Friendly aliens.
Illinois	6,1 and 6,2	May hold for six years, at the end of which time the alien must have conveyed the realty to a bona fide purchaser for value or must have become a citizen of the United States in order to continue to hold the land beyond the six years.
Maine	87,2	
Maryland	3,1	Friendly aliens.
Massachusetts	184,1	
Michigan	11,813	
Minnesota	8076	Unless the alien has declared his intention to become a citizen of the United States he may not acquire any land or interest therein exceeding 90,000 square feet.
Nebraska	76-502	Aliens may take for five years. This does not apply, however, to land in towns, or land necessary for manufacturing establishments.
Nevada	6365	All aliens may take by purchase the same as citizens except Chinese.
New Jersey	Aliens, sec. 1, p. 39	
New York	51:10	Friendly aliens.
North Carolina	192	
North Dakota	5256	
Ohio	8589	
Pennsylvania	471	Limited to 5,000 acres, or land having a net annual income of $20,000.
Rhode Island	4246	

[1] Citations are to code provisions unless otherwise indicated.

South Carolina	8907 & 7790	Limited to 500 acres.
South Dakota	263	
Tennessee	7187	
Utah	29 Utah 443	
Vermont	25 Vt. 433	Friendly aliens.
Virginia	66	Friendly aliens.
West Virginia	3541	
Wisconsin	234.22 & 234.23	If alien is nonresident he is limited to 320 acres.

TABLE 2

STATES PERMITTING ONLY THOSE ALIENS ELIGIBLE TO CITIZENSHIP UNDER THE LAWS OF THE UNITED STATES TO ACQUIRE LAND BY PURCHASE

State	Citation
Arizona	2782
California	General Laws, Act 261, sec. 1
Florida	Dec. of Rights, 18
Idaho	23-101
Kansas	Supp. to Rev. Stat., 67-701
Louisiana	Constitution XIX, 21
Montana	Supp. to Rev. Codes, 3043.2
New Mexico	Constitution II, 22; and Comp. Stat. 117-116
Oregon	19-101

TABLE 3

STATES PERMITTING ONLY ALIENS WHO ARE RESIDENTS OR ALIENS WHO HAVE DECLARED THEIR INTENTION TO BECOME CITIZENS OF THE UNITED STATES TO ACQUIRE LAND BY PURCHASE

State	Citation	Remarks
Arkansas	Constitution II, 20	Any resident may acquire as a citizen. If alien is a nonresident he must be eligible to citizenship; Act 249 (1925), sec. 1.
Connecticut	5055	Any resident and citizen of France may acquire as a citizen. A nonresident may acquire quarry property; 5056.
Indiana	14709	Any alien who is a declarant may acquire as a citizen.
Iowa	Constitution I, 22	Any resident may acquire as a citizen. Nonresident may acquire land in corporate limits of any town, or lands not to exceed 320 acres.
Kentucky	334 & 337	Any alien who is a declarant may acquire as a citizen. If the alien is a resident but not a declarant he may acquire and hold land for 21 years.
Minnesota	8076	All aliens are permitted to acquire up to 90,000 square feet, but only declarants may acquire in excess of this area. See Table 1.
Mississippi	2121	Any resident may acquire as a citizen.

Missouri	592	Any alien who is a declarant may acquire as a citizen.
New Hampshire	213,19	Any resident may acquire as a citizen.
Oklahoma	8451	Any resident may acquire as a citizen.
Texas	167	Any resident may acquire as a citizen. But in towns all aliens may hold lands.
Washington	Constitution II, 33	Any alien who is a declarant may acquire as a citizen.
Wyoming	Constitution I, 29	Any resident may acquire as a citizen.

TABLE 4

STATES PERMITTING ALL ALIENS, WITHOUT DISTINCTION, TO TAKE
REAL PROPERTY BY DESCENT

State	Citation	Remarks
Alabama	6071	
Colorado	130	
Delaware	Rev. Stat., 3194	
Florida	Laws, 1933, Chap. 16, 103, sec. 29	
Georgia	97-303	Friendly aliens.
Illinois	6,1 & 6,2	May hold for six years, at the end of which time the alien must have conveyed the realty to a bona fide purchaser for value, or have become a citizen of the United States in order to continue to hold the land beyond the six years.
Indiana	14709 & 14710	Only aliens who have declared their intention to become citizens of the United States may take by descent as fully as citizens; see Table 6. All aliens, declarants or otherwise, may take by descent. But a nondeclarant may hold land thus acquired only five years and then must convey the property or become a naturalized citizen.
Iowa	10214	All aliens may take by descent; but nonresident aliens may hold such property only twenty years. To hold beyond that time it is necessary that such aliens become residents of the state. See Table 6.
Kentucky	334 & 338	All aliens may take by descent, but only an alien who has declared his intention to become a citizen may continue to hold as a citizen. A nonresident may hold any land acquired by him through descent for eight years. See Table 6.
Maine	87,2	
Maryland	3,1	Friendly aliens.
Massachusetts	184,1	
Michigan	11813	

Minnesota	8076	
Missouri	590 & 592	
Montana	Rev. Codes 7088 and Supp. to Rev. Codes 3043.4	If a nonresident, he must appear in five years to claim the property. If the heir is an alien who has declared his intention to become a citizen of the United States he may continue to hold the same as a citizen, but if the alien is not a declarant he may hold only for twelve years. See Table 6.
Nevada	6365	All aliens may take by descent the same as citizens except Chinese.
New Jersey	Comp. Stat., Aliens, sec. 3, p. 39	Friendly aliens.
New York	51:10	Friendly aliens.
North Carolina	192	
North Dakota	5759	
Ohio	8589	
Oklahoma	11317 & 8452	Nonresident aliens may only hold the property for five years.
Pennsylvania	461	
Rhode Island	4246	
South Carolina	8907	
South Dakota	717	
Tennessee	7187	
Texas	170 & 167	All aliens may take by descent but must sell in five years if they are not (a) bona fide residents, (b) declarants, (c) citizens of nations having a common land boundary with the United States, (d) citizens of nations which permit citizens of the United States to hold land in fee.
Utah	101-4-24	
Vermont	25 Vt. 433	Friendly aliens.
Virginia	66	Friendly aliens.
Washington	10584	All aliens may acquire by descent. A declarant may continue to hold as a citizen, but an alien who is not a declarant may hold only for twelve years. See Table 6.
West Virginia	3541	
Wisconsin	234.22 & 234.23	

TABLE 5

STATES PERMITTING ONLY ALIENS ELIGIBLE TO CITIZENSHIP TO TAKE REAL PROPERTY BY DESCENT

State	Citation	Remarks
Arizona	987	The alien shall have five years to become a citizen of the state and take possession of such property, or shall have five years to sell the same before it shall be forfeited.

California	General Laws, Act 261, sec. 1 & Supp. of 1933, Probate Code, 1026	If the eligible alien is a nonresident, he must appear and demand the property within five years.
Idaho	23-101	
Kansas	Supp. to Rev. Stat. 67-701.	
Louisiana	Constitution XIX, 21	
New Mexico	Constitution II, 22 & Comp. Stat. 117-116	
Oregon	19-101	

TABLE 6

STATES PERMITTING ONLY RESIDENT ALIENS AND ALIENS WHO HAVE DECLARED
THEIR INTENTION TO BECOME CITIZENS OF THE UNITED STATES TO
TAKE LAND BY DESCENT

State	Citation	Remarks
Arkansas	Constitution II, 20, & Act 249 (1925), sec. 1	Residents may take the same as citizens. But if the heir is a nonresident, he must be eligible to citizenship.
Connecticut	5055	Residents may take as citizens. Similar treatment is extended to citizens of France "so long as France shall accord the same right to citizens of the United States."
Indiana	14709 & 14710	All aliens may take by descent. Declarants may take as fully as citizens. Nondeclarants may take by descent but hold the same only five years.
Iowa	10214	Residents may take as citizens. Nonresidents may hold only twenty years.
Kentucky	334 & 338	Must be resident and declarant to take as fully as a citizen. A nonresident heir may hold for eight years.
Mississippi	2121	
Montana	Rev. Codes 7088 & Supp. to Rev. Codes 3034.4	If a declarant, may hold as a citizen. If a nondeclarant, may hold only for twelve years.
Nebraska	76-502	Resident can take by descent, but only hold for five years.
New Hampshire	213-19	Resident may take by descent as a citizen.
Washington	10584	Declarant may hold as a citizen. A nondeclarant may hold only for twelve years.
Wyoming	Constitution I, 29	May take as a citizen.

TABLE 7

STATES PERMITTING ALIENS, WITHOUT DISTINCTION, TO TAKE REAL PROPERTY BY
DESCENT, BUT WHICH PLACE RESTRICTIONS UPON THEIR TAKING BY PURCHASE

Florida
Minnesota
Missouri
Wisconsin

TABLE 8

TREATIES CONCERNED WITH ALIEN ACQUISITION OF REALTY BY DESCENT*

(a) Those permitting heirs who, because of alienage, cannot enter into possession of realty to dispose of it and remove proceeds within the time noted in the "Remarks" column.

Name of State	Date	Article	Citation	Remarks
Prussia	1785	X	8: 88	Reasonable time.
Spain	1795	XI	8: 144	Reasonable time.
Prussia	1799	X	8: 166	Reasonable time.
Colombia	1824	IX	8: 310	Three years.
Central America	1825	XI	8: 326	Three years.
Hanseatic Reps.	1827	VII	8: 370	Three years.
Prussia	1828	XIV	8: 384	Reasonable time.
*Brazil	1828	XI	8: 392	Three years.
Chile	1832	IX	8: 435	Three years.
Russia	1832	X	8: 448	Time fixed by laws of the country; if no time fixed then reasonable time.
Venezuela	1836	XII	8: 470	Three years.
Peru-Bolivia	1836	VIII	8: 489	Three years.
Sardinia	1838	XVIII	8: 520	Reasonable time.
Ecuador	1839	XII	8: 538	Three years.
Hanover	1840	VII	8: 556	Reasonable time.
Portugal	1840	XII	8: 566	Same as Russia (1832).
Hesse-Cassel	1844	II	8: 818	Two years.†
Württemberg	1844	II	8: 588	Same as Hesse (1844).
Bavaria	1845	II	9: 827	Same as Hesse (1844).
Saxony	1845	II	9: 830	Same as Hesse (1844).
Nassau	1846	II	9: 850	Same as Hesse (1844).
Hanover	1846	X	9: 865	Reasonable time.
Oldenburg	1847		9: 868	Declaration of accession to Hanover treaty (1846).
Swiss Confederation	1847	II	9: 903	A term not less than three years.
Mecklenburg-Schwerin	1847	X	9: 918	Reasonable time.
Austria-Hungary	1848	II	9: 945	Two years.†
Guatemala	1849	XI	10: 878	Three years.
Hawaiian Islands	1849	VIII	9: 979	Reasonable time.
*Swiss Confederation	1850	V	11: 590	National treatment in states permitting aliens to hold realty; in states not so permitting, such time as laws of the state will accord.
Peru	1851	XV	10: 932	Three years.
Brunswick and Luneburg	1854	II	11: 602	Such term as permitted by the laws of the state.

* Treaties marked (*) in force.
† Term may be reasonably prolonged.

*Bolivia 1858	XII	12:1010	Longest period allowed by the law.
Venezuela 1860	V	12:1146	Longest period allowed by the law.
Dominican Rep. 1867	V	15: 476	Longest period allowed by the law.
Nicaragua 1867	VIII	16: 553	Same as Swiss (1850).
Salvador 1870	XXVIII	18: 738	Same as Swiss (1850).
Orange Free State ... 1871	III	18: 750	Such term as law allows.
*Great Britain 1899	I	31:1939	Three years.†
*Guatemala 1901	I	32:1945	Three years.†
*Spain 1902	III	33:2107	Three years.†
*Canada 1921		42:2147	Declaration of accession to British treaty of 1899.
*Germany 1923	IV	44:2135	Three years.†
*Hungary 1925	IV	44:2443	Three years.†
*Esthonia 1925	IV	44:2380	Three years.†
*Salvador 1926	IV	46:2820	Three years.†
*Honduras 1927	IV	45:2620	Three years.†
*Latvia 1928	IV	45:2643	Three years.†
*Norway 1928	IV	47:2138	Three years.†
*Austria 1928	IV	47:1879	Three years.†
*Poland 1931	IV	48:1507	Three years.†
*Free City of Danzig .. 1934		48:1680	Declaration of accession to Polish treaty of 1931.

(b) Those permitting aliens to obtain realty by testament or *ab intestato* and to dispose of the same *at their will.*

Name of State	Date	Article	Citation
*New Granada 1846	XII	9: 886	
Salvador 1850	XII	10: 893	
Two Sicilies 1855	VII	11: 644	
Peru 1870	XII	18: 703	
Salvador 1870	XII	18: 730	
Peru 1887	XI	25:1449	

(c) Those permitting aliens to obtain realty *ab intestato* without being obliged to obtain letters of naturalization. No mention is made of disposing of the realty within any specified time.

Name of State	Date	Article	Citation	Remarks
France 1778	XI	8: 18	
Sweden 1783	VI	8: 64	
France 1800	VII	8: 182	
Sweden-Norway ... 1827	XVII	8: 354	Revived Art. VI of Swedish treaty (1783).

TABLE 9

TREATIES PERMITTING THE CITIZENS AND SUBJECTS OF THE CONTRACTING
PARTIES TO PROCURE HOUSES AND WAREHOUSES FOR COMMERCIAL,
RESIDENTIAL, AND OTHER PURPOSES

Name of State	Date	Article	Citation	Remarks
Great Britain	1794	XIV	8: 124	Hire and possess.
Greece	1837	I	8: 498	Rent and occupy.
Two Sicilies	1845	VI	9: 836	Occupy.
Hanover	1846	X	9: 864	Hire and occupy.
Mecklenburg-Schwerin	1847	X	9: 918	Hire and occupy.
Hawaiian Islands	1849	VIII	9: 979	Occupy.
*Swiss Confederation	1850	I	11: 587	To have establishments, to possess warehouses.
Two Sicilies	1855	VI	11: 643	Occupy.
*Bolivia	1858	III	12:1004	Occupy.
Venezuela	1860	III	12:1144	Hire and occupy.
Haiti	1864	VI	13: 713	Hire and occupy warehouses. No mention of dwellings or houses.
Dominican Rep.	1867	III	15: 475	Same as Haiti (1864).
Peru	1870	II	18: 699	Occupy.
*Italy	1871	II	17: 846	Hire and occupy.
*Tonga	1886	III	25:1441	Rent, occupy and improve lands and erect dwellings, offices, and warehouses thereon.
Peru	1887	II	25:1445	Occupy.
Japan	1894	II	29: 849	Own or hire and occupy houses, manufactories, warehouses, shops and premises which may be necessary for them, and lease land for residential and commercial purposes.
Japan	1911	I	37:1504	Own or lease and occupy houses, manufactories, warehouses and shops, to lease land for residential and commercial purposes.
*Siam	1920	I	42:1928	Own or lease and occupy houses, manufactories, warehouses and shops, to lease land for residential, commercial, religious, and charitable purposes and for use as cemeteries.

* Treaties marked (*) in force.

*Germany 1923	I	44:2133	Own, erect or lease and occupy appropriate buildings and to lease lands for residential, scientific, religious, philanthropic, manufacturing, commercial and mortuary purposes.
*Hungary 1925	I	44:2441	Same as Germany (1923).
*Esthonia 1925	I	44:2379	Same as Germany (1923).
*Salvador 1926	I	46:2818	Same as Germany (1923).
*Honduras 1927	I	45:2618	Same as Germany (1923).
*Latvia 1928	I	45:2641	Same as Germany (1923).
*Austria 1928	I	47:1877	Same as Germany (1923).
*Poland 1931	I	48:1507	Same as Germany (1923).
*Free City of Danzig .. 1934		48:1680	Declaration of accession to Polish treaty (1931).

TABLE 10

TREATIES PERMITTING ALIENS TO ACQUIRE REALTY WITHOUT CONTAINING
THE QUALIFICATION THAT IT SHALL BE FOR RESIDENTIAL,
COMMERCIAL, OR SIMILAR PURPOSES

Name of State	Date	Article	Citation	Remarks
Salvador 1850		III	10: 891	Shall have the power to purchase and hold lands, and all kinds of real estate.
*France 1853		VII	10: 996	Enjoy national treatment in possession of realty in states of the union whose laws permit it.
*Argentina 1853		IX	10:1009	In whatever relates to acquiring and disposing of property of every sort and denomination they are to get national treatment.
Salvador 1870		III	18: 726	Shall have power to purchase and hold lands and all kinds of real estate.
Corea 1882		VI	23: 720	Shall be permitted to rent premises, purchase land, or to construct residences or warehouses in all parts of the country.

* Treaties marked (*) in force.

APPENDIX C

PAYMENT OF BENEFITS UNDER WORKMEN'S COMPENSATION
LAWS TO NONRESIDENT ALIEN DEPENDENTS[1]

(A) STATES IN WHICH NO BENEFITS ARE PAYABLE TO NONRESIDENT
ALIEN DEPENDENTS

State	Citation	Remarks
Alabama	7572	
New Mexico	156-120	
South Dakota	9458 (8)	

(B) STATES IN WHICH LESS THAN EQUAL BENEFITS ARE PAID

State	Citation	Remarks
Arizona	1438 (A)	60% of the amount otherwise payable.
California	Act 4749, sec. 14	Presumption of dependency does not extend to nonresident aliens. If dependency exists in fact, then equal treatment is given.
Colorado	8146	1/4 of the amount otherwise payable.
Delaware	30 Laws of Del., Chap. 203, 3193s sec. 112	Only to widows and children and limited to 1/2 amount otherwise payable. Nonresident alien widowers, parents, brothers, and sisters specifically denied compensation.
Georgia	114-413 (c)	Compensation to dependents not citizens of or residing in United States or Canada at time of accident is limited to $1,000.
Idaho	43-1104	50% of amount otherwise payable. If the country of which the alien beneficiary is a citizen does not extend benefits to Americans in as favorable degree as the Idaho law, then alien shall receive no compensation.
Illinois	48-144 (j)	Alien dependents not residing in the United States or Canada are limited to spouse, children, and parents, and compensation is 50% of amount otherwise payable.

[1] Citations are to state codes unless otherwise indicated.

Iowa	1392 (6)	Same as Idaho above.
Kansas	44-510 (2)	Amount paid nonresident alien dependents shall not exceed $750.
Kentucky	4903	Nonresident alien widows and children only are considered dependents and the compensation is limited to 1/2 the amount otherwise payable.
Maine	Chap. 55, sec. 2. VIII	If dependent resides outside United States or Canada compensation is 1/2 amount otherwise payable.
Michigan	8421	Dependents residing outside the United States and Canada, compensation limited to 66-2/3% of amount otherwise payable.
Montana	2893 to 2897	Dependents limited to spouse or children and to amount ranging from 40% to 50% of that otherwise payable. No compensation is payable to nonresident beneficiary whose government excludes United States citizens from equal benefits.
Nevada	2706 (8)	60% of amount otherwise payable.
Pennsylvania	Laws of 1915, Act 338, sec. 310	Nonresident alien widows and children only are entitled to compensation and at 2/3 of the amount otherwise payable.
Utah	42-1-68	Alien dependents residing outside the United States, or its dependencies, or Canada receive compensation not to exceed 1/2 of the amount otherwise payable.
Virginia	1887 (39)	Alien dependents residing outside the United States or Canada are limited to $1,000.
Washington	7675 & 7684	Same as Idaho above.
Wyoming	124-106-7 (k)	Beneficiaries under the Act do not include alien dependents residing beyond the jurisdiction of the United States except widow, sons under 16, daughters under 18, or parents; limited to 33-1/3% of amount otherwise payable.

(c) STATES EXTENDING EQUAL TREATMENT

Connecticut	5235	The law makes no distinction between those who are presumed to be dependents, as to whether they are nonresident aliens or otherwise. But if the deceased shall have in this state some person or persons who are dependent in fact, the commissioner may, in his discretion, cause an equitable apportionment.
Indiana	139 N. E. (1923) 684	There is no provision in the law on the subject but this case holds that nonresident aliens are not barred from the benefits of the law.

Maryland	Art. 101, sec. 36	Equal treatment is extended only to widows, children, and parents.
Massachusetts	118 N. E. (1918) 942	Same as Indiana above.
Minnesota	4284	
Nebraska	48-122 (4)	Same as Maryland above.
New Jersey	162 Atl. (1932) 891	Case holds that New Jersey law extends equal treatment to nonresident alien dependents.
New York	66:17	Compensation to aliens not residents (or about to become nonresidents) of the United States or Canada shall be the same as provided for residents, except that dependents in any foreign country shall be limited to surviving wife and children, or if none of them, to surviving parents.
North Carolina	8081 (tt)	Same as New York above.
Ohio	1465-107	
Oklahoma	7291	
Oregon	49-1817	Same as Maryland above.
Tennessee	6888	
Texas	8306-17	
West Virginia	2535 (10g)	Equal treatment extended only to widow, invalid widower, child under 16, invalid child over 16, or posthumous child.
Wisconsin	102:51 (4)	

APPENDIX D

[1] Citations are to code provisions unless otherwise indicated.

TABLE OF CASES

BIBLIOGRAPHY

I. Documentary Material

Annuaire de l'Institut de Droit International. Vol. 35, pt. 2, Paris, 1929.
Foreign Relations of the United States. Washington. (As cited.)
State Codes. (The latest editions of all of the states of the United States, as cited.)
State Session Laws. (As cited.)
United States Code Annotated. Saint Paul, 1928.
United States House of Representatives, Report No. 1546, 75th Cong., 1st Sess., Washington, 1937.
United States Internal Revenue Code, 1939. Washington, 1939.
United States Senate, Report No. 2156, 74th Cong., 2d Sess., Washington, 1936.
United States Session Laws, Statutes of the United States of America. Washington, 1935.
United States Statutes-at-Large. Washington. (As cited.)
United States Treasury Regulations. Washington. (As cited.)
United States Treaty Series, No. 920. Washington, 1937.

II. Books

Adams, C. F., *The Works of John Adams.* 10 vols., Boston, 1850-1856.
Bemis, S. F. (ed.), *American Secretaries of State and their Diplomacy.* 10 vols., New York, 1927-1929.
Borchard, E. M., *The Diplomatic Protection of Citizens Abroad.* New York, 1927.
Brierly, J. L., *The Law of Nations.* London, 1928.
Clark, J. P., *Deportation of Aliens from the United States to Europe.* New York, 1931.

Downey, E. H., *Workmen's Compensation*. New York, 1924.

Dunn, F. S., *The Protection of Nationals*. Baltimore, 1932.

Fauchille, P., *Traité de Droit International Public*. 2 vols., Paris, 1925.

Hall, W. E. (ed. A. P. Higgins), *International Law*. 7th ed., London, 1917.

Headlam-Morley, A., *The New Democratic Constitutions of Europe*. London, 1929.

Hill, C. E., *Leading American Treaties*. New York, 1922.

Howell, R., *The Privileges and Immunities of State Citizenship*. Baltimore, 1918.

Hyde, C. C., *International Law Chiefly as Interpreted and Applied by the United States*. 2 vols., Boston, 1922.

Kelsen, H., *Das Problem der Souveränität und die Theorie des Völkerrechts*. 2d ed., Tübingen, 1928.

Lauterpacht, H., *The Function of Law in the International Community*. London, 1933.

——, *Private Law Sources and Analogies of International Law*. London, 1927.

Martin, C. E. and George, W. H., *Representative Modern Constitutions*. Los Angeles, 1923.

McBain, H. L. and Rogers, L., *The New Constitutions of Europe*. New York, 1922.

Moore, J. B., *A Digest of International Law*. 8 vols., Washington, 1906.

——, *International Arbitrations*. 6 vols., Washington, 1898.

——, *Principles of American Diplomacy*. New York, 1918.

Niboyet, J. P., *Manuel de Droit International Privé*. 2d ed., Paris, 1928.

Nielsen, F. K., *International Law Applied to Reclamations*. Washington, 1933.

Oppenheim, L. (ed. A. D. McNair), *International Law*. 4th ed., 2 vols., London, 1926-1928.

Pillet, A., *Principes de Droit International Privé*. Paris, 1903.

Steinbach, P. A., *Untersuchungen zum Internationalen Fremdenrecht*. Bonn, 1931.

Tiffany, H. T., *The Law of Real Property*. Enl. ed., 3 vols., Chicago, 1920.

Van Vleck, W. C., *The Administrative Control of Aliens*. New York, 1932.

Verdross, A., *Die Einheit des rechtlichen Weltbildes.* Tübingen, 1923.

Wilson, G. G., *International Law.* 9th ed., New York, 1935.

III. ARTICLES AND MONOGRAPHS

Carroll, M. B., "The Development of International Tax Law." 29 *American Journal of International Law,* 586-597 (1935).

Fachiri, A. P., "International Law and the Property of Aliens." *British Year Book of International Law,* 1929, 32-55.

Frankfurter, F. and Corcoran, T. G., "Petty Federal Offenses and the Constitutional Guaranty of Trial by Jury." 39 *Harvard Law Review,* 917-982 (1926).

Harper, F. V., "Due Process of Law in State Labor Legislation." 26 *Michigan Law Review,* 599-630; 763-789; 888-905 (1928).

Kelsen, H., "Théorie Générale du Droit International Public." 42 *Recueil des Cours de l'Académie,* 121-349 (1932).

Kuhn, A. K., "The Supremacy of Treaties over State Laws in Respect to the Intestate Estates of Aliens." 26 *American Journal of International Law,* 348-351 (1932).

Kunz, J. L., "The 'Vienna School' and International Law." 11 *New York University Law Quarterly Review,* 370-421 (1934).

McClure, W., "A New American Commercial Policy." *Columbia University Studies in History, Economics and Public Law,* Vol. 114, No. 2 (1924).

Page, T. W., "The Earlier Commercial Policy of the United States." 10 *Journal of Political Economy,* 161-192 (1901).

Powell, T. R., "The Workmen's Compensation Cases." 32 *Political Science Quarterly,* 542-569 (1917).

Root, E., "The Basis of Protection to Citizens Residing Abroad." 4 *American Journal of International Law,* 517-528 (1910).

Thomas, J., "La Condition des Etrangers et le Droit International." 4 *Revue Générale de Droit International Public,* 620-645 (1897).

Verdross, A., "Règles Générales du Droit International de la Paix." 30 *Recueil des Cours de l'Académie,* 275-503 (1929).

———, "Les Règles Internationales Concernant le Traitement des Etrangers." 37 *Recueil des Cours de l'Académie,* 325-406 (1931).

Williams, Sir J. F., "International Law and the Property of Aliens." *British Year Book of International Law, 1928,* 1-30.

Wright, P. Q., "The Enforcement of International Law through Municipal Law in the United States." *University of Illinois Studies in the Social Sciences,* Vol. 5, No. 1 (1916).

IV. Notes

"Constitutionality of Legislative Discrimination Against the Alien in His Right to Work." 83 *University of Pennsylvania Law Review*, 74-82 (1935).

"Workmen's Compensation." 11 *Minnesota Law Review*, 57-65 (1927).

INDEX

Adams, John, 20 f.

Bayard, Thomas F., 17
Buck, Charles W., 17

Central American Court of Justice, 6
Copyright. *See* Property rights of aliens in American municipal law
Courts. *See* International customary law; Jury de medietate linguae; Jury service; Jury trial; National treatment provisions in United States treaties

Employment, alien's right to, 119-143
    Exploitation of public domain, 133-136
    Ordinary occupations, 119-128
    Public Works, 128-133
    State Workmen's Compensation Laws, alien's rights under, 137-142
    See also International customary law; National treatment provisions in United States treaties

Fachiri, Alexander P., 14

Hill, Charles Edward, 35, 43
Hughes, Charles Evans, 39
Hyde, Charles Cheney, 38

Institute of International Law, Draft Convention (1929), 2, 14
International customary law, rights of aliens under, 1-18
    Access to courts, 15
    Arbitrary arrest and imprisonment, 4-6

Gainful employment, 15, 16
Inviolability of domicile, 8
Minimum standard of treatment, 1, 3, 4, 18
National treatment, 1, 16-18
Property rights, 9-14
Punishment of nationals for crimes against aliens, 7, 8

Jury de medietate linguae, 145-151
Jury service, aliens and, 144, 145
Jury trial, alien's right to, 151, 152

Kelsen, Hans, 15

League of Nations, Report of Committee of Experts quoted, 1
Livingston, Robert R., 20

MacGregor, G. Fernández, 7

National treatment provisions in United States treaties, 19-44
    Access to courts, 32-34
    Acquisition of real property, 25, 26
    Charges upon ships, 41
    Discrimination in governmental purchases, prohibition of, 41, 42
    Employment, 23-25
    Enter, travel, sojourn, 22, 23
    Equal treatment in matter of cargoes, 39, 40
    Illegal search and seizure, 26, 27
    Inheritance and transmission of property, 34-38
    Liberty of conscience, 38
    Load and unload parts of cargo, right to, 40, 41